RAMEN OTAKU

RAMEN OTAKU

Mastering Ramen at Home

—

SARAH GAVIGAN with Ann Volkwein

AVERY

an imprint of Penguin Random House
New York

AVERY

an imprint of Penguin Random House LLC
375 Hudson Street
New York, New York 10014

Most Avery books are available at special quantity
discounts for bulk purchase for sales promotions,
premiums, fund-raising, and educational needs.
Special books or book excerpts also can be created to
fit specific needs. For details, write SpecialMarkets@
penguinrandomhouse.com.

ISBN 9780735220065 (hardcover)
ISBN 9780735220072 (ebook)

Printed in the United States of America
10 9 8 7 6 5 4 3 2 1

Book design by Ashley Tucker

This book is dedicated to the otaku, the obsessed, the lovers of ramen. The magic that surrounds this dish cannot be explained in words. It drew me in and gave me a new vocation. The ramen otaku who come to eat at our shop, this book is for you.

To my daughter, Augusta, and my husband, Brad, for taking this journey with me.

TABLE OF CONTENTS

FOREWORD

I've been eating noodles my entire life: ramen, udon, soba, lo mein, chow fun, naeng myun, kal gook su, bun cha. Noodles comfort me; noodles nourish me. I firmly believe that noodles will prolong my life. Noodles are my obsession, but they are not precious. They don't belong in the rarified world reserved for such delicacies as sashimi or kurabota. Noodles are not about precision, they are about emotion. Ramen, more than any other noodle, is a bowl of comfort steaming with umami, salt, fat, and the memories of my youth. We've all slurped. From the ubiquitous instant ramen in college to the busy artisan ramen shops that make you wait on line for an hour, from New York to Tokyo. They never disappoint. They leave you happy and sated.

The days of instant ramen are behind us. The secrets to making real ramen from scratch are available to every home cook, thanks in no small part to Sarah Gavigan. What sets her apart from so many other ramen masters is that she is happy to share her craft and her secrets with the world. To demystify the process just enough to encourage us to try this at home. Because it is worth every effort, every minute of tending to a long-simmering broth, every ounce of your focus to skim and slice and boil an egg. Good cooking is simple. It is never easy or convenient, but it is simple. Follow a clear set of recipes—don't try to improvise or make adjustments. Just be a student and follow the recipes and your reward will be the best bowl of ramen that ever came out of your kitchen.

The first time I had Sarah's ramen was at her home in Nashville. On a lazy weekday evening, I drove down from Louisville. A group of us sat around the kitchen shooting the shit while Sarah carefully tended to a giant pot of broth and an armful of ramen noodles. Her husband, Brad, was telling stories. Nikki Lane was strumming on a guitar. It was a clear night and a southbound breeze was rushing in through the open window. The aroma of the ramen broth was intoxicating. I expected to have good ramen. I didn't expect to have a bowl of ramen that rocked me to my core. It was deep and expressive and flavorful to the point of excess. It smelled of Japan and tasted of the South.

We think of ramen as a Japanese tradition. But traditions don't stand still and they defy easy answers. There are ramen traditions taking root all over America. And I am excited by the transformations that happen when these traditions wash up on our shores. When they simmer and spread through a network of Japanese chefs throughout Los Angeles to land in the inquisitive mind of a young music executive who doesn't even know that her destiny will be intertwined with this centuries-old tradition. And when she brings these techniques to Nashville and starts feeding the hungry crowds in the American South, a new tradition starts to bloom. One that is singularly unique and yet respectful at the same time. It is delicious. It is different. It is Otaku.

Residents of Nashville have long known how good her ramen is. And now Sarah is sharing her secrets in these pages that represent a decade of dedication and obsession. I can't tell you how excited I am for this book to make it out there in the world. She is going to empower an army of home cooks to make ramen at home. The right way. She will educate a generation of cooks to obsess over broth and pork belly and mazemen. I am smiling just imagining all the steaming bowls of ramen that will be taking over the home kitchens across America. Slurp away.

CHEF EDWARD LEE

MY JOURNEY TO BECOMING RAMEN OTAKU

I am Sarah Gavigan. I was raised in Columbia, Tennessee, an hour south of Nashville, and spent nearly twenty years in Los Angeles before my husband and I relocated to Nashville with our daughter in 2010. That's where this story begins. But first, a bit about how I got here.

One day, I realized I am ramen otaku.

The word *otaku* has many meanings. To the older generation in Japan, otaku isn't a compliment—it refers to someone obsessed (usually with anime or ramen), with no outside life. A serious geek. In the U.S. the term has crossed over to become a badge of honor, referring to a geek or nerd who embraces their obsession with intense verve. For me, it's ramen. But what does it really mean to be otaku? It means I will go to great lengths for a great bowl of ramen. Why? Let me explain.

In Japan, you'll find groups of otaku kids (and adults) hanging around ramen shops, chattering about every last detail of the bowls within. There are magazines the size of a Sears catalog to describe only some of the shops in Japan. Some otaku even go so far as to create costumes that represent their favorite anime characters, who often eat ramen. I, however, am not your typical otaku. I'm an Italian American wife and mom, raised in rural Tennessee, who spent seventeen years in Los Angeles working in the film and music industries. I discovered ramen in my twenties, and professional cooking relatively recently, just after I said a bittersweet good-bye to my career and life in California and moved back to Nashville. I had no idea I was ramen otaku until I found myself boiling fifty pounds of pork bones in my backyard at two a.m. But perhaps it shouldn't have been such a surprise, after all . . .

All through my twenties and thirties, while living in the City of Angels, I became increasingly obsessed with food. I trawled the famed Santa Monica Farmers Market on Wednesdays with an extra coffee in my hand, peeking over the shoulders of the city's great chefs—people like Ludo Lefebvre, Neal Fraser, Suzanne Goin, and Joaquim Splichal—with naive curiosity. I had a move: "Hey, Chef, want a coffee?" I would ask. When they said yes, I'd hand over the extra cup and ask, "So what are you going to do with that?" gesturing toward whatever produce they were holding.

I was always in search of new ingredients to cook in the wood-fired oven that my husband built in our backyard in Venice Beach. I hosted twenty-person-plus dinner parties with my best friend, Jennifer, who supplied specialty foods to restaurants all along the West Coast. We'd spend a week planning our menu and several days cooking. No ingredient was out of our reach. Jennifer was the kind of friend who would call me and say, "Would you be offended if I gave you a twenty-pound tuna loin for your birthday?" No, I most certainly would not be!

If I wasn't working, I was traveling to all corners of the city in search of my next great meal, with Jonathan Gold's book *Counter Intelligence* (the veritable guide to ethnic food in LA) in my car at all times. This was the late 1990s, when ramen was not even a discussion yet, except in college dorms—there was no trend to speak of. I was often the only white person in any shop I visited. Yet Jonathan directed my attention toward Santouka, a Japanese chain that has a stall in the food court of a Japanese grocery store called Mitsuwa, just up the street from my house in Venice. It quickly became my own personal wonderland.

By otaku standards, Santouka's ramen is not the bowl to beat, yet to this day it's the version against which I measure all other ramen. My favorite there was shio, or salt-flavored ramen, with a silky tonkotsu broth, clouded with pork fat that coated my lips as I slurped. The noodles were always perfectly cooked—not too soft—and the toppings were simple slices of roast pork chashu and thinly sliced scallions. One bowl in, and I was hooked—Santouka quickly became my local go-to.

I was grateful for it. My nonstop career as a music and film agent often left me stressed out, hungover, or beat down, and ramen was my cure. At night I would wine and dine clients at the hippest new restaurants in New York and LA, all the while thinking about the bowl of ramen I would inhale the next morning. Ramen became my refuge. I would show up in the morning at Santouka in LA, or Ippudo in New York, full of eager questions for my servers, who seemed perplexed by my disheveled appearance and slightly annoying curiosity for what is essentially considered highly revered fast food in Japan. Now, I say "fast" only for the speed at which the food is being consumed. Nothing is "slower food" than ramen, as you will soon discover. At home, I began dragging my friends and family farther and farther afield in search of my next great bowl. My husband and I often set out on weekend food crawls through the Asian enclaves around greater Los Angeles with our young daughter in tow.

I began to acquaint myself with different styles of ramen: rich, milky, pork-based tonkotsu broth, creamy white chicken paitan, light and clean shio. I learned how important it is to begin eating ramen immediately, as it degrades the longer it sits; and I watched and learned how to properly "crush" a bowl—take in the aroma first, a sip second, and then slurp your noodles loudly. The sound of slurping became the real indicator that I was in the right shop. I was, in short, beginning my journey as a ramen otaku, and I didn't yet know how far it would take me.

In 2010, my husband and I made the difficult decision to leave our lives in LA and move to my hometown, Nashville. I wasn't particularly happy about it, but we were facing the realities of the economic downturn, and there simply wasn't the work opportunity there once was for us in California. Plus, we wanted a smaller city to raise our then six-year-old daughter in, so Music City it was. The move was harder on the three of us than I had imagined it would be—life in a small city in the South was worlds apart from the international hub of Los Angeles. I didn't have much work, or many friends, but the worst was the absence of ramen, which had become my security blanket. Suffice it to say, I was not at my emotional best.

I spent two years preaching the gospel of ramen to my fellow Nashvillians, who met

me largely with blank stares. Eventually, my restlessness and ramen cravings turned into threats to start making it myself. "Well, when are you going to stop talking about it and start making it?" asked Miranda, a local restaurateur in Nashville.

That was all I needed to hear. It was time to stop feeling sorry for myself, and start getting to work.

The very next day, I drove straight to Porter Road Butcher, looked the guy dead in the eye, and asked for fifty pounds of pork bones, proudly announcing that I was about to make tonkotsu ramen. Again, a blank stare. *No matter,* I thought. *How hard can it be? It's just boiling bones.* Little did I know just how much I had to learn.

In those early days, the only sources of instruction available to me were YouTube videos of Japanese ramen shops and DVDs friends had given me of televised ramen competitions, along with a few articles I found here and there that didn't tell me anything about how to make the broths or create the tare (liquid seasoning). Lack of information plus lack of any real culinary training in a city that has few to no Japanese restaurants made my goal a daunting one. In Japan, ramen chefs apprentice for years with a master and are notoriously tight-lipped with their recipes, and no one knew anything about ramen for hundreds of miles in any direction from Nashville. So my first few attempts at broth were pretty simple: Dump bones in pot, fill with water, and boil until the marrow started to leach out, which took about fourteen hours. The result? About ten quarts of murky, dirty broth that smelled not unlike the inside of a gym sock. I refused to give up, though, and in fact, I loved every minute of those early days.

My Pop-Up . . . and the Tweet That Changed the Game

Soon, I began to make plans to host a pop-up ramen dinner of my own. Sure, I'd never worked in a restaurant; no, I didn't go to culinary school; and it's true that I had never cooked for more than forty people at once. But none of that fazed me. I started to refine my broth technique, and invest in better equipment to get the job done. That involved buying not only a heavy-bottomed fifty-gallon stockpot (to keep the bones from burning) but also a propane turkey burner upon which to heat said pot in my backyard and a massive second freezer (that lived in my newly renovated dining room) to house my finished broth.

I'd start cooking my broth in the morning, and kept it cooking until the wee hours of the next morning, tending to the giant vats while the rest of my house slept. I remember one very early morning, around two a.m., I went to bail my stock from the backyard in my vinyl gloves and rubber apron, looking like a mortician. I tried to move 150 pounds of liquefied pork fat and boiling water off the stove to strain it. As I worked, I felt the pot handles begin to slip out of my hands, and visions of melting the lower half of my body flashed before me. With adrenalized strength, I recovered my stance and secured the pot. My heart was beating so fast I could hear it, but all that mattered was saving the stock. Things were getting weird, but I had a pop-up to prepare for, and I couldn't stop now.

While I was gearing up for the pop-up, I began hosting an informal series of ramen tastings at my house for friends and family, where I worked out the kinks of the rest of my bowl: the tare, or seasoning that gives the broth its flavor; the toppings, like roasted pork and soft-boiled eggs stained in soy sauce; and even a few of my own inventions, like cast-iron chicken and shredded pork confit, aka pulled pork. This was when I began to develop my own style of ramen, one that's firmly rooted in my Southern surroundings. The other important event during this period was the arrival of Erik Anderson, the chef at the then newly trending Catbird Seat, to my house to taste my ramen—before I'd ever even served a bowl of it to the public.

"Hey, this is pretty good," he said. I was shaking too hard underneath the table to really do anything other than pelt him with questions about how to make a fatty stock broth. His response was simple: "I don't know much about ramen stock, but I would think you would want to use a pressure cooker." I brushed off his suggestion, as I had never seen anyone do that before. "Do you mind if I tweet a picture of this from the Catbird Seat account?" he asked. Mind? I most certainly did not! I was floored that an award-winning chef was in my house, eating my ramen, and telling me he thought it was good enough to publicly endorse.

"COMING SOON: The best bowl of ramen Nashville has ever seen!"

The moment that tweet went out, my life was changed forever. Erik's tweet had pushed me out of the nest. I went from underground to aboveground in a matter of moments. Soon after his post was up, it was re-tweeted by tons of local press—word travels fast in a town like Nashville, especially about something that had basically never been seen there before. I was excited and slightly nauseous all at the same time. I was now fully committed, and there was no backing out—it was time to serve my ramen to the public.

I set the official date for my first pop-up, and 225 tickets sold in less than a week. Erik Anderson continued to be a giant support, helping me find cooks, and Kevin Ramquist, another local chef, was kind enough to let me cook broth in his kitchen. Two hundred twenty-five presold bowls meant eighty-four quarts of broth, requiring roughly two hundred pounds of bones. This was no small operation, and apart from Kevin's borrowed stove for extra broth, I was running the whole thing out of my house.

I tackled my prep with the vigor I had been taught in the film industry. I made lists upon lists, complete with timelines and schedules. Once my broth was strained and ready to go, it had to be stored. No one restaurant had enough room in their walk-in refrigerator for all my broth, so I put one container here, one there. I had a map that looked like a game of Twister to tell me where it all was.

The day before the event, the cooks showed up at my house looking ready for war with their knives and whetstones. I set them to work, and had prep running smoothly, when the doorbell rang. It was a photographer from *Food & Wine*, asking to shoot my ramen on behalf of Erik, who had apparently selected me as one of his top five picks for the best food in Nashville. Was I really being featured in *Food & Wine* before I had even sold my first bowl? Apparently, yes.

The event came and went in a blur, and it was a massive success. Looking back a few days later, I realized that I had loved every second of this crazy thing. And I was moved by it, too: I'll never forget the look on the face of one guest as he ate my ramen, because I knew what it meant to him. You see, a few weeks before the dinner, an older gentleman contacted me about tickets, asking if this was indeed the "Japanese-style ramen" that he had eaten some fifty years ago while stationed in Japan. I served him and his wife personally, quickly running to watch him from behind the kitchen door as he reached for his spoon and chopsticks. First he took a moment to close his eyes and take in the aroma, next a sip of broth, and then finally a giant slurp of noodles. He set both his hands back on the table, straddling the bowl, closed his eyes and let his head tilt back a little, then smiled. I literally began to weep. I had actually done it. I had rung the memory bell for this man, fifty years after his last bowl of ramen. At that moment I knew—not only was I doing this, but I was made to do this.

After that first night, I started hosting ramen pop-ups at restaurants and markets all over town, sometimes serving up to 450 bowls of tonkotsu in one night. Meanwhile, I was prepping everything in my house, creeping around the backyard propane burner to tend to my broth while my family slept, unaware. I'd already bought a giant second freezer that had nowhere to live but the middle of the house, but it soon became clear that I couldn't go on prepping ramen in my home forever.

Eventually I found a commercial kitchen in a nondescript strip mall in East Nashville and started working there, much to the relief of my family. Now I could really get serious about my production and the consistency of my pop-ups.

Around this time, I took the opportunity to enroll in an intensive ramen education course at Sun Noodle (the noodle company that supplies me and most top ramen shops in America) Ramen Lab in New Jersey. I had decided to wait a year to learn as much as I could on my own—I wanted to make my own mistakes before taking the leap. I believed that because of my general lack of culinary training, I had to rely on the skills I did have, which were research and knowing how to talk to people. The chefs I befriended along the way were all French trained, and now I can say with certainty that making ramen stock is the complete inverse of making a French stock. I can recall more than a few times when I had the chance to chat with very accomplished chefs about ramen, who usually met me with the same blank stare that I had grown used to from all my friends. But a few came back with the same suggestion that Erik Anderson had made: use a pressure cooker to make the stock. Again, I refused this idea at first, as it challenged fifty-plus years of ramen culture. But when I attended "ramen school" at Sun Noodle, the ideas all crystallized.

At the Sun Noodle factory—really a warehouse outfitted with a small kitchen—I met Master Chef Shigetoshi "Jack" Nakamura aka Naka, who taught me the traditional methods for making broth. Not just tonkotsu but also the golden chintan chicken stock and the rich, creamy chicken broth called paitan that I had rarely eaten, let alone made. When I got back to Nashville, I started incorporating what I'd learned at Ramen Lab into my menu, playing around with new bowls that reflected my background and Southern surroundings—a roasted-lemon chicken paitan, for example, that nods to my Sicilian heritage while staying true to the traditional Japanese techniques for broth and seasoning.

Meanwhile, the building that housed my kitchen sold to a new owner, and he approached me about putting a restaurant in the space. I came up with the idea of turning the entire place into a sort of culinary incubator for new and emerging chefs, called POP. This concept tapped into a crossroads of my skills and my needs. POP allowed me to keep my commissary kitchen for ramen, and use my networking and marketing skills to invite chefs and restaurants to do pop-ups in the space. The first theme the new owner desired? A ramen restaurant. My ramen restaurant. Which was awfully convenient, given that I was prepping everything right there in the kitchen.

Otaku South opened at POP in May 2014 for a one-year residency. Subsequently, Otaku found a permanent home in the Gulch area of Nashville, opening as a standalone restaurant in December 2015 as Otaku Ramen. When I began this journey, Nashville was on its way to becoming nationally recognized as a killer food city, but there was little ramen to be had. I reveled in bringing my obsession to my new city of Nashville. I wanted to help introduce my friends and neighbors to the "traditional" ramen you'd see in Japan, but I quickly realized that there's no such thing—ramen is always shaped by its surroundings. So I started making bowls that reflected what Nashville knows and loves: smoked pork, pickled vegetables, hot chicken, and more. I developed my own personal style—one that's rooted in Japanese technique but distinctly tied to my own *terroir*.

I continued to make ramen at home, and started developing some tips and tricks that made it much easier for the home cook than what I had been taught along the way. My experiments revealed that my chef friends were right—a pressure cooker can produce golden chintan chicken stock and some of the creamiest paitan broth in one-tenth the time it takes on the stovetop. I reverse engineered my favorite tare, or the liquid seasoning that gives each ramen its distinct flavor, out of pantry ingredients that keep indefinitely. And I built relationships with my vendors, which I will share with you to make sure you can get the proper ingredients, such as the noodles themselves.

Now, I'm ready to share my story and my recipes. Some of the greatest ramen chefs in the world are tight-lipped with their knowledge, but I'm a Southern girl who likes to talk and likes to teach. I'm proud of what I've learned and what I've built, and I want to show home cooks that it is indeed possible to make great ramen in their own kitchens. And I want to inspire a new generation of ramen otaku to create their own personal ramen styles, built upon their own tastes and surroundings.

In this book, we'll cover the fundamental techniques and recipes that all ramen otaku should master as a foundation, then I'll share some of my favorite recipes for unique craft ramen that build off those fundamentals.

Home Cooks Rule the World

Let's get something straight: First and foremost, I am a home cook. The life of being a professional cook and chef came to me at the age of forty-two. I got here by being a passionate and obsessed home cook. And I am and always will be a cookbook-aholic. It's where you dreamily get to be transported into someone's mind and kitchen. My goal with this book is to give you the knowledge I have gained by searching, testing, tripping, sliding—and getting back up.

There are a few immutable aspects we have to work with in home kitchens as opposed to a commercial-grade kitchen. Heat is the biggest. The power of a gas range in a restaurant is roughly ten times what is legally allowed in a home kitchen, and ramen broth requires high heat. We will get to that. All stovetops are not created equal and time can be a cruel mistress, but you will have options.

This book is the culmination of four years of work to understand the shrouded world of ramen. The complete bowl is broken down here into its elemental parts. And I provide the recipes and methods that come straight from our ramen shop combined with the knowledge you need to replicate our bowls and then go on to create your very own signature bowl of ramen.

I, a chef and the author of this book, am not a wizard with magical powers used to make a secret and unreplicable bowl of ramen. I am the Alice in Wonderland of ramen. I fell down the rabbit hole and fell in love with the process of making and serving ramen.

If you are here, then I bet you will, too.

Is This Ramen Authentic?

Before we move forward, I want to tackle the prickly topic of authenticity. If you have not figured this out yet, I am a middle-aged white woman who is a mother and a wife. I am not Asian, and I am not a tattooed chef with a flat-bill hat and a bunch of punchy things to say on Instagram. I don't slaughter my own pigs. Does that stop me from making a great bowl of ramen? No. Does being Asian ensure that you know how to make a great bowl of ramen? Well, in a word: NO.

Let's explore the value of the word through our country's own greatest food export, the cheeseburger. Does the cheeseburger belong to the United States? Sure, we gave birth to

it, gave it a name, and it is our national food, but let me tell you I had the best hamburger of my life in Japan. Does that make it less authentic? Nope, it just makes it GOOD.

The literal dictionary definition of the word *authentic* is "at its origin." So what is the origin of ramen as we know it? Japan. I am not in Japan and I am going to bet the majority of ramen you have consumed was not in Japan, either.

Japan has a world of ingredients and dizzying methodology that makes food grown and made there unique to that country. We cannot make Japanese ramen in the U.S., nor are we going to attempt to. But what we are going to do is take the foundation of how to make a bowl great, how to create umami and flavor and texture from the origins of the motherland, using (largely) ingredients from your surroundings. So take the word *authentic* out of your vocabulary right now. It won't serve you here. *Good, tasty,* and *balanced* are the only words we need.

American Ramen Godfather Chef Ivan Orkin gave me an incredible piece of advice once on how to handle criticism of my ramen. "You just have to understand that I will never know what you taste." He's right. It's a simple thing to come to terms with, which is that everyone has different tastes for salt and flavor. I am going to teach you what you need to know to make these decisions for yourself.

GO EAT A BOWL OF RAMEN

This food is important for many reasons that I will tell you about in this book, but also for no other reason than it's simply magic. I want to make a recommendation before diving into the book: Go eat at a proper ramen shop. Have that experience by yourself. Just watch the whole process, put your phone down, take off your glasses (that's what I have to do), tuck your napkin into your shirt, and dive in. Tackle the noodles first, a little broth, more noodles, toppings, then drink the rest. Don't stop till that bowl is finished. Do not check your phone. Do not waver from this bowl of ramen. The simple task of eating a bowl of ramen with only your own thoughts can change the course of your day. Okay, I know that sounds a bit lofty, but just do it.

Why? Because if you want to learn how to make ramen, it must be a love affair. This is

チャーシュー 醤油らーめん $12.95
Chashu(Pork) Soy Sauce Ramen (M)
15 チャーシュー ちび 醤油らーめん $11.95
Chashu(Pork) Soy Sauce Ramen (S)
チャーシュー 大盛 醤油らーめん $13.95
16 Chashu(Pork) Soy Sauce Ramen (L)
$10.45
※サンプルは普通盛りです
A sample is the MEDIUM size (M)

醤油らーめん
Soy Sauce Ra

12 ちび 醤油らー
Soy Sauce Ra

13 大盛 醤油らー
Soy Sauce Ra

※サンプルは普通
A sample is the M

チャーシュー 味噌 らーめん (M) $12.95
Chashu(Pork) Miso Ramen (M)
チャーシュー ちび 味噌 らーめん (S) $11.95
Chashu(Pork) Miso Ramen (S)
25 チャーシュー 大盛 味噌 らーめん (L) $13.95
チャーシュー(Pork) Miso Ramen (L)
ザルは普通盛り size (M)

味噌らーめん (M) $9.45
Miso Ramen (M)
22 ちび味噌らーめん (S)
Miso Ramen (S) $11.45
23 大盛味噌らーめん
Miso Ramen (L)
※サンプルは普通盛りです
A sample is the MEDIUM size (M)

HOW TO CRUSH A BOWL OF RAMEN

No one likes to be told how to eat, but it's vital here. A hot bowl of ramen has a rapid expiration point. The moment you begin to cook your noodles, the clock is ticking. Whether at a ramen shop or when serving it at home, you must know that the moment a complete bowl of ramen hits the table, it is time to consume. Cease conversation, no need to wait for everyone else to get his or her food (that's an American thing, I think), just dive in. This is how I have been taught to eat a bowl of ramen.

1 Take in the aroma first. Stick your nose over the top of the bowl.

2 Taste the broth, but do not stir the ramen.

3 Eat your noodles. SLURP. I can't say it enough.

4 Have a bite of your toppings in between big slurps of noodles.

5 Drink your remaining broth.

This should all happen in ten minutes or less. It's all-consuming as you eat, and it may not be what you are used to, but to have the true experience, you have to crush that bowl. It deserves your attention, and after you read this book and serve a bowl of your hard-loved ramen to your friends, you will have joined the club. It is truly a labor of love that should be appreciated in its consumption.

not a dish you are going to whip up one afternoon for friends that night. It will take days of planning and cooking to create the foundation for something that will be served and consumed in a matter of minutes. But this food, this dish, is rewarding in ways other foods are not, and that is what we will focus on here. For a beloved food that's been shrouded in so much mystery it's actually incredibly simple, but guess what? It's not easy.

Ramen is both simple and complex—like your grandmother's spaghetti Bolognese or your family's beloved chili recipe. There's endless room for differentiation. Very much like a professional cook, you may have to try some of these recipes over and over before you get it right. What does a professional cook have over a home cook? Mileage. The tested, retested, and retested muscle memory of making the same thing over and over and over again. So maybe we take out that last over, but be prepared—if you want to learn how to make ramen, you're going to do it over and over again. And hopefully, if you're the kind of person I think you are, you are going to enjoy it. A lot.

When I talk to friends who like to spend hours hovering around their kitchen like I do, stock always comes up. "I love making stock," said my friend and ramen chef Jessica Benefield of Two Ten Jack. "It's passive time, but it really takes a constant touch." What she said reminded me of the time I complimented a family friend on her hot-water cornbread (literally wet cornmeal fried up in a cast-iron skillet with lard and hot water). "Oh, it's easy, but you have to get it just right!" she said as she wagged her finger at me.

That's what making broth on a stovetop is like. It can be strangely therapeutic. But that being said, let's get real: it's not every day that I yearn for ramen or have twenty-four hours to babysit a wildly bubbling cauldron of bones and water. I am giving you a couple of methods: stovetop and pressure cooker.

A Word on Stovetop versus Pressure Cooker

Stock is the centerpiece of a bowl of ramen, so almost all our equipment needs (see page 48) fall into this category. The biggest choice to consider before you begin this book is whether you will make your stock on the stovetop or in a pressure cooker. There are merits to each method, which I go into greater detail about in the "Stock" chapter. The short answer is time. How much time do you have to spend? It's an honest question, and luckily both methods are great. The fun part is you can do both.

UMAMI

The hunt for true umami is a lifelong journey as a chef and cook. Yet, it is a natural occurrence in some foods, and you have experienced it—even if you didn't know what it was. In layman's terms, umami is the irresistible savoriness that defines the word *flavor*. As elusive as that may sound to Western ears, scientifically speaking, there is actually an amino acid called glutamate that signals the presence of umami. In fact, the term *umami* (うま味) was coined by a Japanese scientist (shocker, I know) named Kikunae Ikeda in 1908, and directly translated, it means "pleasant, savory taste." It's the so-called fifth taste.

I'll admit, the term always felt very out of reach for me as a home cook. What is umami? How do I make it or get it? Someone takes a bite out of a dish and says, "Oh, wow, that has such incredible umami." Am I a jerk if that really annoys me? It's not a flavor, and it's not salty, sweet, or bitter. It's the fifth taste. Parmesan cheese has umami, as do tomatoes, seaweed, soy sauce, but what does that mean exactly?

I know it means that I will eat Parm chips till they are ripped out of my hand (the kitchen has to hide them from me; it's become a serious game), but how do I cook dishes that have umami? How do I get my ramen to have umami?

Plus, I bet you are thinking, *Wait a minute. Glutamate—I've heard that word before.*

Yep, that would be monosodium glutamate, aka MSG, aka magical fairy dust, aka

Umami Central. Monosodium glutamate is a salt (created in a laboratory) that has been modified with umami superpowers. Oh, I know you're going to say, "I get a headache when I eat MSG." Maybe, it's possible, but there are many amazing and hilarious debates on the topic. My favorite is Jeffrey Steingarten's perspective in *The Man Who Ate Everything*. (Sidebar: so, so good and funny.) Everyone wants to claim they are allergic to MSG, but I stand with Jeffrey on this one. Just don't overuse it and you won't be allergic to it any more than you are to the other thirty kinds of modified starches and salts that are used in the top one hundred kitchens in the world—down to the family ramen joint. Real talk.

We don't use it much in this book, but I will never tell you not to have some around to pull a tare together at the last minute. Stuff happens, and umami is needed. But if you understand the basics of naturally occurring umami, where to find it, and how to extract it, then your tiny little MSG pot won't get much play at all.

Let me pull the curtain back a little. It's a salt that is modified, but so is your Morton iodized salt. A sprinkle of MSG ain't gonna hurt nobody, but a heaping tablespoon in one bowl of ramen will make you feel like a rabid dog as you eat, as in: *I want all of this right now oh my god it's so good I can't stoooopppp* . . . then you will have cottonmouth and, yes, possibly a headache.

Moderation Is the Key

Just like your grandma has a trick for fixing that broken sauce that she won't tell anyone about, I give you permission to fiddle around with MSG, in moderation. I am going to go on record and say that yes, we use MSG in small amounts at the shop to boost flavor and create consistency. We tell people this when they ask us if we use any and tell us they are "allergic" and they have no physical response ever.

UMAMI TEST

I do this test for every line cook who comes into my kitchen, and I want you to do it as well. Buy a small bag of MSG. Go home and put a pinch on a plate next to a pinch of salt (kosher and/or sea) and a pinch of black pepper and white pepper. Now lick your finger and taste each one on the very tip of your tongue. MSG comes last. Now do it again in the middle of your tongue. The taste of umami lives in a specific place on the middle back of your tongue. Get it? This is how you will know if umami is present in your food: when you taste it and your palate reacts in that same spot. The only way to understand it is to taste it. Do with that knowledge what you will, but now you know.

The best way to describe it is to say that it's the taste that makes everything else taste

KOMBU
FOR DASHI AND SOUP

HIJIKI
FOR TOPPINGS AND SALADS

better. A great bowl of ramen is built on this principle. But how in the heck do you make it happen? How does natural umami happen?

It's not magic, which without clear explanation it can seem to be; it's pure science. Let's geek out for a minute.

Some foods have what is called glutamate, which is literally an amino acid, and your body loves those little guys. It can be naturally present, like in kombu (seaweed) or it can manifest through fermentation (soy sauce, fish sauce), and it has been used to boost the flavor of foods since the Byzantine Empire.

What this all means to a bowl of ramen is that you will use combinations to create a bowl with balance and umami. That is the hallmark of a great bowl. Not too salty, not too sweet, not too sour or bitter . . . right in the middle. Many of the methods and ingredients used in this book when combined will create or aid in the presence of umami in your food. Now you can see the combos, and this is where layering comes into making a great bowl.

UMAMI CHART

Certain foods have concentrated amounts of one or several of these aminos. Now, here's the jam: When you combine two or more of these aminos together, BAM, you get the presence of umami. The major bonus, outside of making your taste buds supremely happy, is that all these amino acids are packed with goodness for your body, which helps make ramen broth an anti-inflammatory food. (Intrigued? More about this in the "Stock" chapter.)

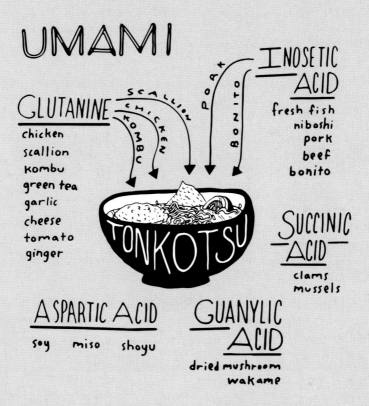

UMAMI

INOSETIC ACID
fresh fish
niboshi
pork
beef
bonito

GLUTANINE
SCALLION
CHICKEN
KOMBU
PORK
BONITO
chicken
scallion
kombu
green tea
garlic
cheese
tomato
ginger

TONKOTSU

SUCCINIC ACID
clams
mussels

ASPARTIC ACID
soy   miso   shoyu

GUANYLIC ACID
dried mushroom
wakame

With this umami chart, you have the keys to the kingdom. After four years of chasing umami and learning how to make a great bowl of ramen, I had a good friend put this in front of me and I think I heard birds and angels sing. It's not magic; it's science.

So keep this chart in mind as we move forward, and once you take your ramen-chef training wheels off, this will be your guide to making the ultimate bowl of umami. Not to mention the ninja skills it's going to give you in general as a cook.

RAMEN BASICS

You are about to fall down the rabbit hole of ramen. Ramen is one of those foods that is riddled with mystery and strange confines. When I began this journey to learn how to make ramen in 2012, there were only bits of information here and there online about how to actually make the entire dish. It's even harder to define, as you are about to find out. These methods go against anything you may have learned about stock and broth to date. The secrets of ramen have been closely guarded since the boom began in Japan in the 1950s. My goal with this book is to present ramen making in as clear a manner as possible. It may not be easy, but it is systematic—a layering process that you can learn. The elements stand alone but work and play together.

Treat this book like a novel at first: curl up in bed with it, and then plot your plan. I know it's difficult to read a whole cookbook all the way through, but ramen is not just a recipe; it's a cuisine. There's a philosophy around each method and element and how you marry them together. It can be really delicate or really intense. And it's not a one-recipe dish; it's a multiple-recipe dish. You could jump straight to stocks, but in order to really know ramen, you need the complete picture, because every little piece plays a valuable role.

The ingredients are simple—bones + water—but the way you prepare them is everything. You are going to work with new ingredients that can be hard to find, but your old pal Amazon is going to make this part fun and easy. I am even going to give you different ways to use these new ingredients to add to your overall cooking arsenal.

Depending on what you're serving, you can prepare some of the elements weeks in advance or days in advance. I will encourage you to master the basics and then create, not just imitate. Ramen is a really fun canvas.

Once you understand the elements, the possibilities are endless, and you will start to look at creating a bowl of ramen the way I do. For example, this morning I went to the market in Chinatown in New York City. The first things I saw were beautiful whole chickens, so I started there. Next thing I was thinking about was, *What flavor do I want my ramen? What style do I want to make, a clear broth or a cloudy broth?* What elements do I need from here? Shoyu today, I thought, so I purchased soy sauce, then the dashi—and then I checked out the vegetables. I saw some nice greens to put on top and a duck egg. I observed a guy bringing in fresh pork and I thought about doing a meatball and saw another guy with fresh duck and thought, *Alternatively, I will make a chintan broth, shoyu flavored, topped with seared duck breast and duck egg, Atjima-style.*

You really can walk through the grocery store or market and progressively build your bowl of ramen. The tare, which is the concentrated seasoning you will use to flavor each bowl, is the epicenter. Then there's the stock, protein, oil, and seasoning. My thought process often goes something like this: If it's spring and still chilly out but I want something light and fresh, I might make a chintan. If I want it to have a little bit more flavor, I'll make a shoyu for it. And then I'll add seasonal spring vegetables, like turnips or turnip greens, which are phenomenal in ramen. My protein could be almost anything. There's the traditional chashu, rolled pork belly, or, for something a little cleaner, I might do grilled shrimp—which is not very traditional at all.

It's all dictated by the seasons and what's available around you. Maybe your butcher doesn't have pork bones that day, maybe he has beef bones, or maybe your skills are up to making a chicken and beef ramen. In the summertime I might still want soup, but I want a completely different flavor profile, as I go more for hot spice in the heat than I do in cold weather. Hearty miso and Sapporo-style ramen come from Hokkaido, the coldest part of Japan, so that appeals to me in the wintertime.

Animal Bones

It all begins with what kinds of bones you can get. You can certainly set out on a mission to make tonkotsu, but if you can't find the right pork bones, it's moot. Find a butcher or meat counter who will work with you, because you will be making an unusual request, and

you may have to call in advance, depending on where you live. In the case of pork, you're going to need them to cut your bones smaller, allowing you to extract all the marrow. It is a waste of time to try to make these broths unless you have the proper base. Chicken is a lot easier and more accessible, so I advise starting there. The method is also a more delicate and sensible way to make a stock. Once you get a feeling for that, then the intensity of making a marrow stock (a paitan) is going to come more naturally to you, especially if you're going with the stovetop method, as it's a long process.

Broth Style

The second decision is what style to make your broth. Will it be chintan (clear soup) or paitan (white soup)? I'm providing the traditional basics here, but you can make either style with any bones—or combination of bones. It's the second flavor layer for your ramen.

I highly recommend committing time in advance to simply make the stock. If it comes out nicely, freeze it, and then you can move on to the other elements.

Ramen Styles

The third decision is what ramen style to use. There are a plethora of styles, as the regional variations have grown well past a few hundred, and after you master the basics, you will undoubtedly create your own style. I cover the main styles in depth later in the book (see page 151). Style and flavor can kind of mean the same thing in ramen, which can be a bit confusing. But as you learn more and play with them more, you will begin to understand their relationship. Tokyo-style shoyu, for example, can be a lighter style, with more emphasis on the bright flavor of the soy; that's the star of the show. But shoyu can also be a flavor; for example, in Wakayama-style there is a tonkotsu broth with shoyu tare, which represents the "flavor."

Flavors

Stock is important, but it is the tare that sets ramen chefs apart. The tares I am teaching you are purposely very simple to allow for your own improvisation. It's all about what you're in the mood for. I believe that the bowl to master first is shoyu, because it encapsulates all the most delicate pieces of making ramen. Tori chintan (clear chicken broth) is the hardest broth to master (I know you are thinking, *What? I already make this broth all the time.* Sure you do, but not like this). The tare is simple to make, but to build this bowl you must understand umami. There's nowhere to hide with that bowl. This is where you will master the balancing act of umami. The essence of ramen, to those who make it, is balance. If you have too much of one thing, it overpowers and throws it all off. But one salt level does not suit all. One flavor, one style does not suit all palates. Your flavor guide might be to re-create a bowl of ramen that you've eaten a hundred times and love. There's good, bad, and revelatory ramen, but honestly I find that people gravitate toward what they've eaten the most. There's no right or wrong, just what your palate likes.

Noodles

One of the first things people ask me is, "Do you make your own ramen noodles?" . . . But they have no idea what goes into that process! One of the keys to making outstanding ramen noodles is having the best flour, milled to perfection. Most U.S. wheat is superior, but the Japanese technology for milling is well beyond American mills, and it makes the noodle smooth. While it requires only three ingredients, the ramen noodle–making process can be ruined simply through a few extra drops of water (ramen noodles are very low moisture) and must be made with a large machine, making it very difficult to integrate into a ramen shop. It is perhaps a bridge I will cross in the future, but right now I put my noodles in the hands of the experts.

But if you are an avid ramen eater who has eaten ramen in various parts of the world, you'll have noticed that there are a variety of different ramen noodles. In my world and in ramen shops it's possible to get very specialized with noodle type, based on the bowl we're making. But I can source my varieties on a commercial level. You'll need to work with what you can find in your Asian market or what fresh noodles you can order. I'm going to teach you how to match your noodles to your broth with the help of my good friends at Sun Noodle.

Toppings

Your final decision for your bowl is what toppings you'd like to feature. Simple is always better. You will have spent a lot of time on your broth and flavor; they are the stars of the show, but the toppings play a wonderful supporting role. Let the main elements stand for themselves; don't overcrowd the bowl. Every single thing that you put in that bowl is going to change the flavor. Sometimes egg and rolled and braised pork belly, aka chashu and scallion, are enough.

HOW LONG DOES IT TAKE TO MAKE A BOWL OF RAMEN?

I think by now you can see that even to make one bowl of ramen is a well-coordinated effort. Can it be done in one day? Yes, one very long day, or you can break it up into a few days. It's up to you. Here is a handy go-to guide on times, to help you make those decisions as you plan your prep.

TARES

Shio	2 to 3 hours
Shoyu	1.5 hours
Spicy Miso	20 minutes
Miso	30 minutes

STOCKS

Chintan	STOVETOP 8 hours • PRESSURE COOKER 3 to 4 hours
Paitan	STOVETOP 9 to 10 hours • PRESSURE COOKER 5 to 6 hours
Tonkotsu	STOVETOP 12 to 14 hours • PRESSURE COOKER 5 to 6 hours

TOPPINGS

Poached Chicken Breast	1 hour
Chicken Confit	Day ahead + 3 hours
Meatball Mix	45 minutes
Chashu	5 hours
Soy Pork Belly	Day ahead + 4 hours
Pork Confit	7 hours
Szechuan Ground Pork	20 minutes

Shiitake Mushroom
牛しいたけ
NT WT. 6 oz.
JAPANESE SHIITAKE MUSHROOMS
NIJIYA MARKET

Red Vein
Sorrel

Sour
Lemon-like
flavor

$3.00 PER BAG

Pantry

The ramen pantry can feel intimidating and specialized, but like all amazing ingredients, once you become familiar with them you will use them in other ways. Spend a little time here and the recipes will seem familiar.

WATER

One might not think that water is special, but when making something as simple and pure as stock with two ingredients, water makes up over half the equation. Much of the water that comes from our faucets is rife with unwanted chlorine and minerals like calcium that can really mess with your flavors. You have options here, from a home filter like a Brita, to going all the way and getting reverse osmosis water at the health food store. At the end of the day, clean water will yield a clean stock with no aftertaste. Tap water can sometimes yield a metallic aftertaste that fights with some of the fermented and dried-fish flavors. It can go so far as to taste like licking the inside of an aluminum can. Yuck. This also pertains to using aluminum pots (see page 48).

SHOYU

Known in America as soy sauce, standard Japanese shoyu (I use Kikkoman, seriously!) is well rounded, while the Chinese version is more intense. I tend to cook with Chinese dark and light soy sauce, and make my tare from Japanese shoyu. If you are really interested in understanding the differences, buy small bottles of all three and taste them side by side; then you can decide what flavor profiles you prefer. There's also a fourth: white soy sauce. It's very expensive when using in volume, but if you have some on hand and really like the flavor, try it. In this book, I reference only the Kikkoman style of shoyu, but don't be afraid to play around with the others. Now, if you have access to high-end shoyu, by all means play around with it. Shoyus are deep and complex and rarely do they taste alike. There are entire books dedicated to this topic.

MISO

You will find insane variations of miso in a good Japanese grocery store, but for these recipes I use simple yellow miso. But don't be afraid to try different types and styles of miso in your tare. When I sub a new ingredient, I make a small batch to see if I like it. Some have dashi built in (conveniently, they usually have a picture of a fish on the label); some have more kombu built in.

DASHI

I call this "sea stock," as we are taking the combination of water, kombu, and dried fish and heating it gently to make strangely flavorless stock. But dashi is the epitome of umami, because on its own, it doesn't taste like much, but when added to a chicken stock, for example, the dashi enhances the flavor of the stock (or just about anything else you add it to; think miso soup). There are many methods and recipes for dashi, but I prefer to use dashi packets, which look like tea bags that you steep in the water to make my dashi. It's not cheating; it's actually very smart. Buy the highest-quality Japanese dashi packets that you can find. I buy awase dashi made by Maruhachi, which has a perfect combination of dried fish and seaweed. Steep according to instructions for perfect dashi every time. Some packs have more MSG than others. I prefer the cleanest I can get, as it's better to add a little MSG at the end of the program than early in the game, for fear of overseasoning. Be a purist when it comes to dashi, play around with different types of dashi or of seaweed, but don't feel bad using instant Japanese dashi, too. They are still way superior to the instant products we have in America. These ingredients have traveled a really long way to get here, so to put them in this state first is not a bad thing. Just as I am giving you license to use MSG in small amounts, instant dashi can be umami insurance. For the first big batch you make at home, make four different kinds of dashi, and when you assemble your bowls, make it four different kinds of ways. I'll say it again—it is a matter of taste; there is no right or wrong.

HONDASHI/MSG

Made by Ajinomoto, the first company to make MSG, HonDashi is freeze-dried dashi with MSG. It's an amazing tool in the kitchen. Like many things, don't abuse it, but it can help get you to umami in a way salt cannot. If you have a stock in which you're using dashi, you can add a bit of HonDashi and you're guaranteed umami. It's an insurance policy. For example, if you're serving a large group something like a thick, fatty, dense paitan and you want to ensure that your flavor profile stays the same in all the bowls, HonDashi is going to be your best friend.

SEAWEED

Kombu is the main type of seaweed that we use in ramen making. It comes in really large leaves. If it's kept in a pantry, well wrapped, it will keep for years. It may seem that you can cut a corner here, but it's important to buy the highest quality you can find. However, it's hard to know what is good quality and what isn't. I recommend Emerald Cove, which sells Pacific kombu, or if you are shopping in an Asian store, look for the largest leaf you can find.

BONITO FLAKES
KATSUOBUSHI
- use in dashi

BONITO HEELS
KATSUO ATSUKEZURI
- use in tare, dashi

MACKEREL HEELS
SABA ATSUKEZURI
- use in tare, dashi

FISH POWDER
KATSUO GYOFUN
- use in ramen

DRIED ANCHOVY
NIBOSHI
- use in tare, dashi

MACKEREL FLAKES
SABABUSHI
- use in dashi

DRIED FISH

There are so many different kinds of dried fish, but for the purposes of this book, we will use these three:

Niboshi
It will sometimes say anchovies and sometimes say sardines on the package, so don't get confused. Niboshi gives you the strongest of fish flavors. If you really want to smell the ocean, you will like it.

Katsuobushi ("katsuo")
The second dried fish we will use is tuna/bonito flakes, or katsuobushi, also called katsuo. I use it for aroma. The flakes are very thin—the thinner the flake, the larger the surface area, and this brings the strongest smokiness to the situation.

Sababushi ("saba")
The second cousin to katsuobushi is sababushi, or mackerel. It's less popular and less strong than katsuobushi but is also used for aroma. I call for both in my Cold-Brewed Dashi (page 97), but you can substitute katsuobushi and you will be fine if you can't find it.

SALT

It's simple—not every salt is created equal, and certain salts perform better in certain situations. In my ramen shop I use 100 percent kosher salt, but I use many different salts at home. The most reliable salt to use is Diamond Crystal kosher salt, and all the recipes in this book are measured using this salt. Believe it or not, Morton kosher salt in the same volume will give you a much stronger, saltier taste. Kosher salt is the most common, affordable, and consistent when it comes to seasoning a broth. Sometimes I use Maldon salt in a tare for the brightness of the salt, but it's very expensive. It's simply up to you and your taste, but you have to pay attention to the dilution, which is why I prefer fine Korean salt when cooking at home. It's like talcum powder with beautiful dilution, which is what you need for a fatty stock to provide an even flavor. Kosher salt adds salinity but not that brightness. Do not use iodized salt, only sea salt or kosher salt. Iodized salt lends a metallic flavor that does not work well in the ramen world.

WHITE PEPPER

White pepper is very prevalent in ramen, for color and presentation, but it also plays well against the fattiness and saltiness. You will see white pepper in any traditional ramen shop; it's always offered. But whether you use it is a matter of taste.

MIRIN

Mirin is a seasoned cooking wine that's important for braising your proteins and building your tare. It's a building block. It has the consistency of a light syrup or a fortified wine; it's the sugar delivery system for your flavor profile—that's why it's great for dressings.

SSM (SOY SAKE MIRIN)

I keep SSM, which is equal parts soy, sake, and mirin, in my refrigerator all the time. I can make anything from braised pork to ponzu or build a tare or make a soy egg with it. It's great in a pinch. My daughter sautéed mushrooms in it the other day, and it was delicious.

SAKE

When cooking with wine, the better the wine, the better the sauce, but this rule does not apply to sake. Buy the cheapest sake you can find for cooking, as it's merely there to create balance, not for flavor or depth. Drink your good sake, cook with the cheaper stuff.

SUGAR

Sugar is to be used only for balance in very small portions. You won't see it called for often in this book, but let's be clear: Ramen is about balance.

GARLIC

Garlic plays a lot of different roles in ramen but not in the way you might think. It's not used in stock and it's rarely used in braising the meats. It's used raw when added to a ramen or in the crunchy, fried form of garlic chips.

GINGER

Generally speaking, ginger adds another layer of flavor for your stock or it's used as a mirepoix for meat and proteins. I also like to add a bit of grated ginger to the top of ramen for an extra kick. I remember the first time I studied with Naka, I noticed that he kept his ginger wrapped in wet paper towels in a ziplock bag on the countertop, at room temperature. When he unwrapped it I could see that the skin was almost translucent—because he'd hydrated it. He told me to chop it thin and stopped me from peeling it. Keeping your ginger hydrated is really important for flavor delivery.

SESAME

I buy untoasted, raw sesame seeds because I think freshly toasted sesame adds an incredible layer of flavor—it smells so good. Sometimes I make a compound of Maldon salt with

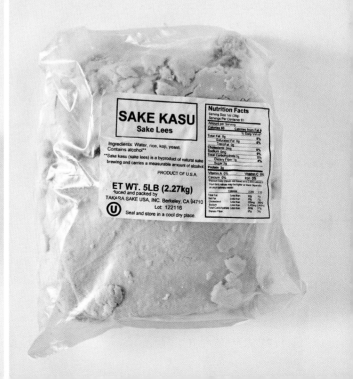

Mits...

KEW...

Mayon...
マヨ...
17...

$4.

KEWPIE
MAYONNAISE

KEWPIE
MAYONNAISE

...PIE
...NNAISE

500g
500g

EXPORT

toasted sesame that is partially ground in my mortar. It's a nice way to top off a bowl. One-quarter of the ramen bowls I'll teach you will call for sesame seeds, so don't be afraid to buy a lot. You may want to make your own sesame paste, in which case toasting them right before you make the paste will be important, as toasting releases the oils. Buy raw and toast for potency.

SESAME OIL

Sesame oil can be used alone or combined with other oils to make a compound oil for drizzling on top of ramen or for making Rayu (page 109).

GOCHUJANG

Gochujang is a traditional fermented chile paste from Korea. It has a lot of depth, the right amount of heat, and can be used for a lot of things. We mix it with miso in the shop to make our spicy miso tare and we mix it with other fermented chiles to make what we call a spice bomb, which can be added to pretty much any ramen to give it heat and spice.

SHIO KOJI

Shio koji is a mixture of fermented rice and salt. It looks a bit like pureed rice porridge, and it contains enzymes that work with proteins to tenderize and enhance umami flavors and add a slight sweetness as they break down starches. It's umami central—and the most well-rounded salt you will ever put in your mouth. I use it for pickling and to enhance dressings, marinades, and proteins. One of my favorite tricks is to take the gnarliest piece of beef I can find, put this on it to marinate for twenty-four hours, then sear it in a pan . . . It tastes like it has ten pounds of butter on it; the meat tastes like Wagyu. You will blow all your friends away when you cook with shio koji, either as a marinade, in a sauce, or as a seasoning—and you can start with my recipe for Koji Chicken Breast (page 123).

SAKE KASU

Sake kasu is the lees left over after sake production. In other words, it's derived from the rice after fermentation, when the sake is strained off. You'll see the magic that happens when you use it as a seasoning; it makes for incredibly well-balanced flavors.

Equipment

This is our guide to equipment. I, like you, always bristle a little at this section because I don't want to buy any more stuff for my kitchen. I will help you weigh the pros and cons.

STOCKPOT

Now look at that—they call it a STOCKpot because it's going to cook food for a long time. So it must have a HEAVY (thick) bottom and it should be stainless steel. Let me explain.

Heavy Bottom

Don't burn the stock! Once you master my chicken stock, you will realize that you have been burning chicken stock your whole life (I had been), so the thick bottom is going to help give your pot the type of even heat it needs to cook steadily.

Stainless Steel

Aluminum is not your friend. I know it's cheap, but it's going to leach chemicals into your beautiful stock, maybe even prevent that golden color, and possibly react by creating a weird aftertaste.

ELECTRIC PRESSURE COOKER

This is the one and only piece of equipment in my house I could not live without. I cannot recommend this investment more for making ramen broth and for a million other things. Why have a slow cooker when you can have a pressure cooker? Using a pressure cooker is a hands-off method of making stock that provides really consistent results (all other elements being the same). The big bonus here is the lack of oxygen in the cooking process. There is a consistent and controlled outcome every time. Your chicken stock will have a deep golden color that you just don't get from the stovetop. It's impressive, and I personally always go with this method at home. You are not a slacker if you use a pressure cooker—you are smart and you will be revered for your golden chicken broth—but let them think you slaved.

A word to those scarred by the memory of an exploding pressure cooker. The new ones are electric with locked lids, 100 percent safe and foolproof when their tops are secured (and they won't allow you to cook unless the top is secure). You hear steam for a few minutes and then it's silent. No rattling or whistling to knock your nerves. You may have seen the Instant Pot ads and Pinterest madness. It's worth every accolade, but any electric pressure cooker will do.

TEMPERATURE GAUGE

Nothing fancy, just a temperature gauge that allows you to check the temperature. Some of these stocks should never be above 190°F. In the ramen shop, we use ones that affix to the side of the pot.

REFRACTOMETER

Not necessary but really fun. I will give you license: After your twentieth batch of stock, if you've taken it that far and you still want to keep going, then pony up three hundred dollars for one of these. I love this tool because it measures the viscosity (liquid thickness) of the stock and tells you when your stock is ready to be pulled off the stove. When used correctly, the refractometer is kind of addicting. This tool will give you the ability to precisely measure one against the other and become a legit ramen master. Not sure if that twenty-five-dollar chicken was worth the money? This will help you decide. The refractometer measures by Brix. One of the great hallmarks of a bowl of ramen is its viscosity. You may like your ramen at a 4, and someone else might like it at a 6. It can help you establish individuality with your ramen. Your stock is not based completely on just flavor; your pork stock will be complete only when the marrow is released, the collagen is melted, and the calcium is leached from bones. It may stay at a 6 for hours, then all of a sudden go to an 8 because that final bit of calcium creates the viscosity that you're looking for. It's these markers the refractometer helps you find and learn. You can find them online or at a brewer's store, for beer making.

Tabelog, the popular website for restaurant listings in Japan, cites that there are over 51,000 ramen shops in the entire country, and 21,000 of those are in Tokyo. For reference, there are 24,000 restaurants in all of New York City.

FINE-MESH STRAINER OR CHINOIS

This is vital for straining broths. Cheesecloth placed in a large strainer works as well.

FOOD-GRADE PLASTIC OR GLASS CONTAINERS

For storing soup in the refrigerator. I suggest glass for stock. If you only have plastic, make sure it's food-grade and only for stock. Your stock will be hot enough to melt plastic.

IMMERSION (HAND) BLENDER OR WHISK

One of the secrets no one tells you: Your favorite ramen shop uses one of these (they just don't show you) to emulsify the stock. It took me four years to uncover that one!

Where to Buy

Planning ahead is key here; it will make the process less annoying. Try these sources in this order.

1. JAPANESE GROCERY STORE

This is the apex and where you will find all that you need for your ramen: a Japanese-owned grocery store. Hit the internet to find one in your city. A good local market will have dried fish, miso, noodles, sake kasu, shio koji, dashi packets—the works—because these are all normal cooking items for the Japanese.

2. ASIAN GROCERY

Large international markets will have some of what you need but not all. You will have to utilize the internet as well to get the more specialty items.

3. GROCERY STORE

You will find vegetables and proteins here but hardly any of the specialty items, though bones may be available here.

4. ONLINE

Almost all your dry goods can be found online. Amazon has a good selection, but the Rakuten Global Market can help as well—it's worth checking out, but note that some of the English translations are not exact. I have found all the dried fish, shio koji, and sake kasu here as well.

Recent statistics show that over a hundred billion servings of instant ramen are consumed worldwide each year.

Document the Process

It's important. The key to making great ramen is to keep doing it, and take notes on each batch so that you can make comparisons. As a home cook, I tend to wing it a lot, kitchen sink it, cook with whatever I have, but when it comes to ramen, I take very detailed notes so that I can continue to hone in on what I prefer. For example, maybe I have a batch of chicken stock where I've used whole chickens (minus the breasts) as opposed to carcasses or cages. Which yielded a richer stock, and which tasted better? My notes reveal all. As I noted earlier, you can construct a bowl as you walk through the store, but after you make it, you will want to leave yourself notes for the next time. You might discover it's worth the fifteen-minute drive across town for that amazing chicken.

SHOYU KOJI	KINZANJITSUKE NO MOTO 30	MUTENKA SHIO KOJI	MARUKOME MISO&EZ MILD CH	MISO & EZ ORIGINAL	HISHIKU SATSUMA MUGI MIS
NIJIYA	NIJIYA	NIJIYA		NIJIYA	NIJIYA
1 /	1 / 10.58OZ	1 /	1 / 13OZ	1 / 13.8OZ	
$5.99	$4.99	$5.99	$4.99	$5.29	$10.

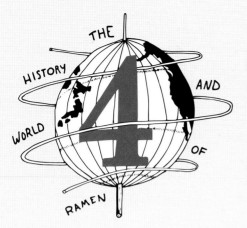

THE HISTORY AND WORLD OF RAMEN

One of my favorite questions to ask people is, "How old do you think ramen is?" Almost every time they respond, "Ancient." Nope, not at all. By Japanese standards, ramen is a modern food and only began to come into popularity post–World War II. The generally accepted history is that the noodle originally came from China. But ramen noodles evolved from a noodle made with kansui, which is basically liquid baking soda, and hold up in scalding-hot broth. It was the most delicious thing people could make out of bone scraps,

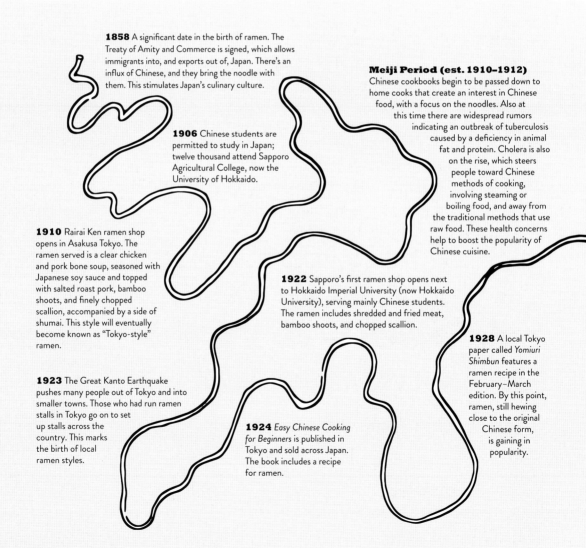

1858 A significant date in the birth of ramen. The Treaty of Amity and Commerce is signed, which allows immigrants into, and exports out of, Japan. There's an influx of Chinese, and they bring the noodle with them. This stimulates Japan's culinary culture.

1906 Chinese students are permitted to study in Japan; twelve thousand attend Sapporo Agricultural College, now the University of Hokkaido.

Meiji Period (est. 1910–1912) Chinese cookbooks begin to be passed down to home cooks that create an interest in Chinese food, with a focus on the noodles. Also at this time there are widespread rumors indicating an outbreak of tuberculosis caused by a deficiency in animal fat and protein. Cholera is also on the rise, which steers people toward Chinese methods of cooking, involving steaming or boiling food, and away from the traditional methods that use raw food. These health concerns help to boost the popularity of Chinese cuisine.

1910 Rairai Ken ramen shop opens in Asakusa Tokyo. The ramen served is a clear chicken and pork bone soup, seasoned with Japanese soy sauce and topped with salted roast pork, bamboo shoots, and finely chopped scallion, accompanied by a side of shumai. This style will eventually become known as "Tokyo-style" ramen.

1922 Sapporo's first ramen shop opens next to Hokkaido Imperial University (now Hokkaido University), serving mainly Chinese students. The ramen includes shredded and fried meat, bamboo shoots, and chopped scallion.

1928 A local Tokyo paper called *Yomiuri Shimbun* features a ramen recipe in the February–March edition. By this point, ramen, still hewing close to the original Chinese form, is gaining in popularity.

1923 The Great Kanto Earthquake pushes many people out of Tokyo and into smaller towns. Those who had run ramen stalls in Tokyo go on to set up stalls across the country. This marks the birth of local ramen styles.

1924 *Easy Chinese Cooking for Beginners* is published in Tokyo and sold across Japan. The book includes a recipe for ramen.

if that was all they had to eat. Ramen has always been an evolution from where we were, where we are, and where we are going, and it will continually change. There is even ramen made out of soy milk now—and it's delicious.

When it comes to food, I am a bit of a history buff. It's amazing to see the time lines illustrating how and why ramen became so beloved in Japan and now in North America.

I really enjoy looking at food through the lens of history, as it gives me a point of reference by which to then create my own version.

Ramen in North America

I didn't realize how young ramen culture was in the U.S. until I began to write this book. Like many of you, I simply thought ramen had been around forever. As you can see by this short time line, ramen is very new here.

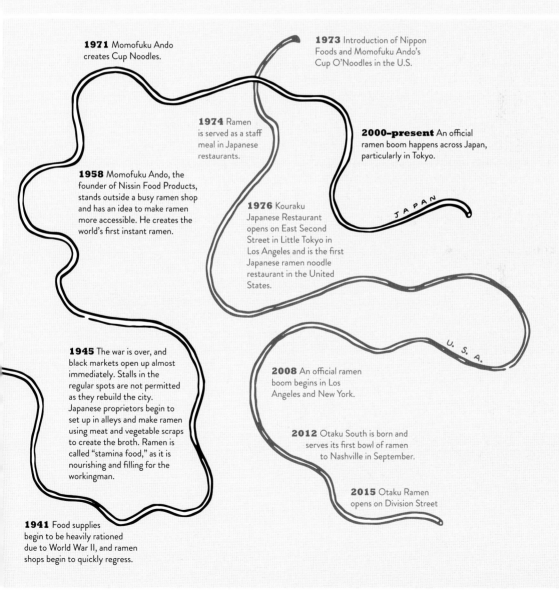

1971 Momofuku Ando creates Cup Noodles.

1973 Introduction of Nippon Foods and Momofuku Ando's Cup O'Noodles in the U.S.

1974 Ramen is served as a staff meal in Japanese restaurants.

2000–present An official ramen boom happens across Japan, particularly in Tokyo.

1958 Momofuku Ando, the founder of Nissin Food Products, stands outside a busy ramen shop and has an idea to make ramen more accessible. He creates the world's first instant ramen.

1976 Kouraku Japanese Restaurant opens on East Second Street in Little Tokyo in Los Angeles and is the first Japanese ramen noodle restaurant in the United States.

JAPAN

1945 The war is over, and black markets open up almost immediately. Stalls in the regular spots are not permitted as they rebuild the city. Japanese proprietors begin to set up in alleys and make ramen using meat and vegetable scraps to create the broth. Ramen is called "stamina food," as it is nourishing and filling for the workingman.

U. S. A.

2008 An official ramen boom begins in Los Angeles and New York.

2012 Otaku South is born and serves its first bowl of ramen to Nashville in September.

2015 Otaku Ramen opens on Division Street

1941 Food supplies begin to be heavily rationed due to World War II, and ramen shops begin to quickly regress.

Ivan Orkin (Ivan Ramen Slurp Shop)

When did you have your first official bowl of ramen?

By my memory it was a bowl of miso in Shibuya. I had probably had ramen before that, but this was my first memory of eating a very, very hot bowl of ramen with my Japanese friends egging me on to slurp even though it was so hot I was very uncomfortable to eat it. It was important to eat it like that. Even in my early twenties it was important to me to eat it the right way; it was when I came to understand the significance of slurping.

Is miso a style you like to make?

I have been known to make miso over the years, and in my eyes the only proper way to make miso ramen is in a wok because really good miso ramen is an emulsification of miso and soup and a healthy dose of pork fat. Heat it at a really high temperature in a wok and it all comes together. In Japan it is a very complex thing to serve because if you don't do it right, it can taste just like miso soup with noodles in it.

What made you want to start making ramen?

That first bowl of ramen I had was in 1987, and then I returned to America a few years later, went to cooking school, and then fast-forward to 2003, when I returned to Japan, and it was the beginning of the ramen boom. Even though ramen had been around for a while, it wasn't until the early 2000s that the country really started getting excited about it, and it really

became this crazy obsession for people. I had lived in America for thirteen years between living in Japan, and the one thing I really could not eat in America was ramen. Now you can eat ramen in many parts of the world, but until Ippudo came to New York in 2008 you really couldn't eat ramen in the States. When I got back to Japan, I was really looking forward to eating ramen; there were so many shops and people were so interested in it. My wife and I started researching a business, and my wife pointed out that all I really wanted to do was eat ramen so why not open a ramen shop.

How did you settle on tori shio as your signature ramen?

I was not working, I was taking care of the kids and during the day I would drive my wife around to props shops for her job as a set dresser and we would seek out all these ramen shops. We were eating a lot of ramen, and as was then and as is now, the most popular style is pork bone ramen, or tonkotsu. I think it's the easiest to understand, it's the junkiest, it's a lot of fun to eat, it's got a lot of fat in it. I love it, but I was forty-four when I went back to Japan and I could not eat fat like that anymore; it just made me feel bad. And then one day we found a shop that served a ramen called a "double soup" and it was a lighter-style ramen. There are many different styles that are a double soup, but it always includes combining two soups and it often includes dashi. The place I discovered had a really rich dashi broth with a clear chicken and pork broth combined and all of a sudden it was much lighter, the flavors were much cleaner, and I didn't feel sick after I ate it. So I started discovering these lighter-style soups. I have a fine dining background and I think the challenge of a shio ramen was really interesting to me. It is the hardest style because good ramen is perfecting a balanced bowl and getting it just right. The cleaner and clearer the soup, the harder it is. I found it very intriguing because there was very little information and very few people serve shio ramen. The whole thing for me was this crazy, interesting challenge. I didn't go to Japan to learn about ramen or open up a ramen shop. I am a lifelong Japanophile who married a Japanese gal and she had a great gig in Tokyo and we both had kids and so we went from New York back to Japan. I was looking for purpose. I had spoken Japanese for thirty-something years and it's my great passion, so the ramen shop was my opportunity to delve super deep into Japanese culture, and the kicker was that it was culinary culture as a tool. It was valuable to be able to do this project in Japan because it really did require a knowledge of Japanese language and culture and cuisine. It was super stimulating.

When you were eating and learning, were people talking about region, and how did that relate to style?

Tokyo is a lot like New York, in the respect that all the best things find their way to Tokyo. In my humble opinion, ramen is really a Tokyo phenomenon. The ramen scene in Kyushu, for example, is really, really different because they have had a ramen scene for much longer and yet it's mostly Hakata-style tonkotsu. I think what happens is that all these styles come to Tokyo and they get synthesized. Ramen is not really a purist food. The reason why I think I had success with ramen in Japan at all is it's one kind of restaurant where there are no rules; there is no rule book. I can walk into a sushi bar, and in one hundred paces I can tell you what kind of sushi it is. A ramen shop, in some ways the less you know the better. When you walk into a shop, it is driven by the owner's persona, charisma, and the kodawari, the thing he has chosen to differentiate his ramen from everybody else's. When I came up with the notion of kodawari, of finding that special ingredient that sets you apart, it was really big, it was gathering steam. I made some of my own choices, I decided to make my own noodles, I used whole wheat flours. I did a lot of things that were very cheffy in my own little world of a ten-seat restaurant. I would assume in Tennessee there are similarities in BBQ. You are driving down the road and all of a sudden there's a dude with a little BBQ on the side of the road. He doesn't know what the fuck anyone else is doing, he only knows he can get this cut of meat and he has this kind of wood to burn and he has this kind of barbecue mop, and he is doing his thing. It could be really good, or he may not know what he's doing and it

continues >

could be really horrible. And that is the beauty of ramen, that there are a certain amount of people doing their own thing. Ramen is one little world that is very different from the rest of Japan because the outliers are the ones who become ramen shop owners.

One of the reasons I love ramen is that there are no rules. If you don't serve that crystal-clear bowl of shio ramen, I know I can get it in another place on another day. I think in the next twenty years we're going to see a lot more ramen. Remember, when I started there was not one thing written in the English language about ramen.

Is shio ramen the style of ramen you could eat every day?

I could actually eat almost anything on my menu every day because I want people to be able to eat it, then go back to work or go out to a movie. When I first started eating ramen, maybe 70 to 80 percent of the bowls I ate made me bloated or gave me diarrhea or put me to sleep. It's fat and salt, it's not something dirty. Maybe, when you're twenty, you can eat that and be just fine. Part of my story is that I started this in my midforties. My epiphany was that I needed to look for a bowl of ramen that was a lighter style. There were people in Tokyo doing pristine bowls of ramen. It's always been an underground sort of thing. All the ramen geeks in Tokyo are eating dashi-based bowls, and those are the ones getting the Michelin stars, but it's not what the majority of people are eating. Most people like a lot of pork fat and lots of chiles and thick chunks of pork belly.

Ramen and barbecue are super similar. I always use this analogy: It's very hard to eat barbecue in a dainty way. You always try to keep your hands clean, but your face and hands get all covered and that's part of the fun. Ramen is the same. I used to marvel that a very pretty girl would come into my 250-square-foot ramen shop in her Chanel and tie her hair back, maybe put a napkin over her blouse and then she would just go to town, her glasses would have speckles of soup and her face would be shiny from the fat, she'd be slurping and making noise and she was cool because she knew when she was eating ramen she was going to enjoy it. For me it's super satisfying to see when people eat ramen they let their hair down a little bit.

Has it been hard to let go of how ramen should be eaten and what a ramen shop should feel like compared to what it is now in the U.S.?

Japan is really different than the States. You have your few serious shops in the States, like the soup Nazi on Seinfeld, my dad would go there years ago and he would say to me that "the soup was so good, so I just kept my mouth shut and got my soup." Japan has a lot of shops like that where you're not allowed to talk or take a picture. It's not a very American thing. I came back to America very humble. I am in the hospitality business, and I want people to eat ramen because I think it is one of the most delicious things in the world. And I love Japan and I want people to connect ramen with Japan, visit Japan, and appreciate Japan. It's my great love.

My mission is to get people to slurp because I think it facilitates enjoying ramen. When you eat a big steaming-hot bowl of ramen, the flavor changes very rapidly. My favorite analogy is if you're a New Yorker, you know that if you go to a coal oven pizza joint, you don't go to the bathroom when the pizza hits the table, even if you have to pee really badly. You wait because you know that when you get back from the bathroom the pizza is not going to taste as good. Same thing—when a Japanese guy gets served a bowl of ramen he's going to eat it as quickly as possible. As the soup cools the noodles soften, when the noodles soften the flavor of flour bleeds into the soup, the fat that is so important in making that bowl delicious starts to congeal and it changes.

What do you think the biggest differences are between ramen in the U.S. and ramen in Japan? Is it the way it's served or the way it's made?

Generally speaking, the best ramen in America is only okay ramen in Japan, except for mine . . . A really delicious burger in Tokyo is really good but not as good as the best burger in the U.S. But I am so impressed with everybody and it's very exciting. And one of the things I fell in love with about ramen is that it's so personal. The one thing that's the same between America and Japan is that people who get bitten by the ramen bug have the same reaction. And everybody has different styles. There's really not that much attitude.

What's the most extreme interpretation of ramen that you have eaten? Can it go too far and break too many rules?

Like I said, there are no rules, so no, it can't break any rules. But there are like three rules in my opinion: Ramen has to be hot and have fat in it. It really should be salty. And the noodles need to marry the soup so that when you slurp, the soup sticks to the noodles and they feel a part of the bowl. Sometimes if you don't choose the right noodles for the broth they're so slippery that you just slurp them up and it's

just like eating flavorless pasta and you have to sip the soup. To me that's a massive fail.

But, at the end of the day, if people like it the argument is over. If I go to a place and I don't like it but I look around and the place is packed and everybody's happy I say, "You know what I don't get it, but you don't always have to get everything." When you're young you think you have to get everything; I keep getting more mature.

What's the ramen secret you wish everyone could know?

The ramen secret is slurp your fucking noodles; it's a ten-minute meal, maybe fifteen. My average eating time for a bowl of ramen is four to six minutes. It's a lot of noodles, and if you eat them slowly, they start to swell and you look at the bowl and think, how am I going to eat all of this? Doesn't happen when you slurp.

Where in the world (outside of Japan) do you see the most exciting ramen being created?

I would say New York, but once again sometimes those are fighting words. I haven't really eaten it anywhere else. Ramen is having a boom in Asia, Hong Kong and Singapore and Taiwan. When I started ten or eleven years ago, there were guys who were already the kings and now they've become legendary. Very flamboyant from the early 2000s to 2011, a lot have been bought out or have expanded into Asia, which is easier for them than coming to the U.S. But as Americans start becoming more comfortable with ramen and go to Japan, it will change; the world is shrinking rapidly and it's fascinating to me. My first book was about saying I didn't get a leg up from anybody, and it was my offering to people to learn a lot from what I write.

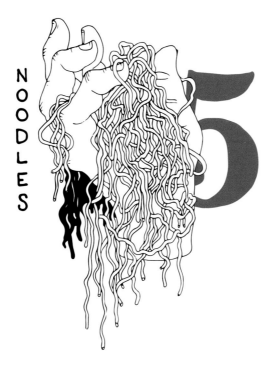

NOODLES

5

The ramen noodle is the heart of the dish, and if you eat a bowl of ramen correctly, it's the first thing you eat. SLURP your noodles first, as they will continue to cook in the broth, and if you waste too much time, eventually they will absorb the broth. As my friend and serious ramen lover Brian MacDuckston said, "The fact that the ramen noodle does and can absorb the soup is one of the things that makes it so wonderful to eat."

The noodle itself is what makes ramen ramen.

I touched on the history of how ramen actually came to be in the "History and World of Ramen" section, but in summation, it all began with the noodle coming over with Chinese immigrants into Japan in the early 1900s. It is the kansui (liquid alkaline salt) added to the noodle that gives it an unmistakable snap to the bite. History says the alkaline noodle came from a small village in China where the water source was alkaline and produced this unique noodle. Without the alkaline salt, it's simply a wheat noodle, otherwise known as white soba.

As Harold McGee wrote in the inaugural issue of *Lucky Peach*, which focused on ramen, alkalinity has a "significant effect on the texture, color, and flavor of the noodle," lending it a yellow hue and a firmness that holds up in hot broth.*

So I think I know your next question. What exactly is alkalinity? I am not a chemist,

---

*McKeever, Amy. "Inside Sun Noodle, the Secret Weapon of America's Best Ramen Shops." *Eater*, 22 July 2014.

"WE GOT ONE HUNDRED TYPE OF RAMEN NOODLE, HONEY!"

It was August 2012, and I had fully committed to my first pop-up, set for September 29. Using well-earned research skills from my film production days, I found Sun Noodle. I had seen their noodle crates in ramen shops and during all the online gawking I had done to learn more from my kitchen in Tennessee. Emblazoned on the sides of all the crates was: Sun Noodle. I discovered that they were based in Hawaii and Los Angeles . . . and I called them up.

"Hi, yes, I would like to speak to someone about buying some ramen noodles for a pop-up ramen event that I have coming up."

Silence . . .

"Yeah, okay, honey, what kind of ramen noodle you want?" asked the lady on the other end of the line. "We got one hundred type of ramen noodle." *Good god*, I thought, *I really know nothing*. She kindly took my number and said she would have someone from sales call me. The next day I got a phone call from a very nice young man who introduced himself as Kenshiro Uki, the vice president of Sun Noodle and the son of the founder. We talked about what type of ramen I was making. The next thing I knew it was time for our pop-up, and the day before the event five cases of noodles showed up on my doorstep, delivered at no charge. Sun Noodle had donated all the noodles to help get me started. They had me at hello.

Sun Noodle immediately provided a friendship and vital working relationship for me as a young ramen chef. Kenshiro was smart in more ways than one. He saw me simply as a young chef. Not as a woman, or a non-Asian woman, but as a chef who was seeking knowledge and with whom he shared a deep love for ramen. And he was happy to share his knowledge.

In 2012 Sun Noodle brought Tokyo's number-one-ranked ramen chef Shigetoshi "Jack" Nakamura (aka Naka) to the U.S. to work directly for them in what they called their Ramen Lab, a place where chefs could come to learn the foundations of ramen. As the ramen industry was growing, there were more and more people like myself looking for knowledge. Bottom line, Kenshiro and Jack set the U.S. ramen market on a path of sharing knowledge instead of hoarding it. That generosity in itself has created a community. They share because it will be better for all of us, as it strengthens the industry, resulting in better ramen chefs and a wider ramen audience.

My relationship with the ramen community, with people like Jack and Yuji Haraguchi (Okonomi, Yuji Ramen) and Kenshiro, has made all the difference in my growth. They understand that there are no secrets or tricks; it all comes down to execution. Even if we all started with the same ingredients, our bowls would be different; everyone has their own touch. Ramen is 20 percent ingredients, 80 percent execution: the particular method you use to make the broth has everything to do with how it tastes.

and chances are neither are you, so for now it's just important to understand that it's a substance that gives the noodles their character, color, density, and flavor. Chemically speaking, it's a potassium and sodium bicarbonate. Kansui is the liquid version, and baking soda the powdered version.

The differences between ramen noodles and regular pasta are:

1. As opposed to the flour used in regular pasta, the flour used by professional noodle makers is finer than talcum powder. It's the fineness of the flour available to them that allows for a really smooth bite on their noodles. This makes ramen noodles impossible to reproduce easily, either in the restaurant or at home, as the only flour you can buy is twice as coarse as what Sun Noodle and other ramen noodle makers use.

2. The addition of the alkaline salt in the ramen dough.

3. The moisture.

Moisture in the ramen noodle is much lower than in pasta, and it varies from noodle to noodle. The lack of moisture is what helps it stand up to scalding-hot broth. In the ramen shop, every time we make a new bowl, one of our quests is to find the perfect noodle to pair it with: thick, thin, wavy, straight, ribbonlike, long, or short. The experience of each bowl is enhanced and enlivened by having just the right noodle to pick up the broth as you slurp.

The process of making ramen noodles is complex and nowhere near as simple as making regular pasta. You can make ramen noodles by hand, but it's not like making Italian pasta, where you simply cut noodles out of sheets of dough. The best ramen machines express the ramen noodles, using calibrated weight to compress the dough depending on the noodle shape and type, and it's the pressure that is the key. Cut yourself a break and go on the Sun Noodle website to order the same ramen noodles that all the best ramen chefs are using across the country. Trust the experts.

Matching Noodles to Your Broth

How do you choose what noodle to use in what soup? Again, no rules, but there are some guidelines that will help you decide if a noodle is well matched to a broth. This mind-set is used by chefs who have hundreds of choices. Yours will be slimmer, but I want to give you the tools to make good choices. The type of soup you are serving will dictate the thickness of the noodle. For example, a tonkotsu is typically served with a thin noodle. A clear soup can be served with a thicker noodle.

The two main factors to consider are slip and chew.

The first main factor is the slip of the noodle as you slurp. Does the noodle slide right into your mouth with some broth and oil? Then it's perfect. The noodle is meant to be not only for bite but also as a delivery system for the broth. The proper noodle will bring some broth with it, which is why you need to SLURP (are you sensing a theme here?).

The other most difficult aspect of the ramen noodle is the chew, but this factor is simply a matter of taste. Do you like your pasta al dente? Same concept.

I remember the first time I saw "soft," "medium," "hard" on a ramen menu to describe how someone likes their noodles prepared. It did not strike me as a very big deal when I was a mere ramen consumer, but when I became a ramen maker, I realized just how difficult that offering is. It's a variation of a matter of seconds in the cooking of that noodle that creates these distinctions. In the shop we do not batch cook noodles the way you might a box of pasta. We have portions that are cooked in separate baskets to ensure each guest gets the same amount. You will most likely be batch cooking, so keep in mind that the noodle will cook for another two to three minutes after coming out of the hot water and before hitting the broth than normal—so better to undercook it by a few seconds and let the broth continue to cook the noodle.

It's fast, so no matter what noodle you choose, I recommend that you make a small batch of the noodle first and test the chew. If you have some broth, tare, and oil, test your noodle in the soup. Think about slip and chew.

So, in summation, here is a basic breakdown of what style of noodle goes with a particular style of ramen. Sun Noodle will be your only bet for finding these variations, and they name their retail line by the style of ramen itself, which makes it easy.

SHOYU OR SHIO / MEDIUM NOODLE / WAVY / MEDIUM CHEW

We use what is called a "Tokyo Wavy" noodle here. It most closely resembles the instant ramen noodle. It's slightly yellow from the alkaline, and wavy to help with its slurpability.

TORI PAITAN / MEDIUM NOODLE / WAVY OR STRAIGHT / SOFT CHEW

Our paitan noodle is a straight white noodle that most closely resembles a white soba noodle. I like it because the chicken fat clings right to it and makes it super slurpable.

TONKOTSU / THIN NOODLE / STRAIGHT / HARD CHEW

We use the thin noodle for all our tonkotsu-based ramen. We cook the noodle quickly so that it has a hard chew the first few bites and then it softens up quickly as it continues to cook in the bowl.

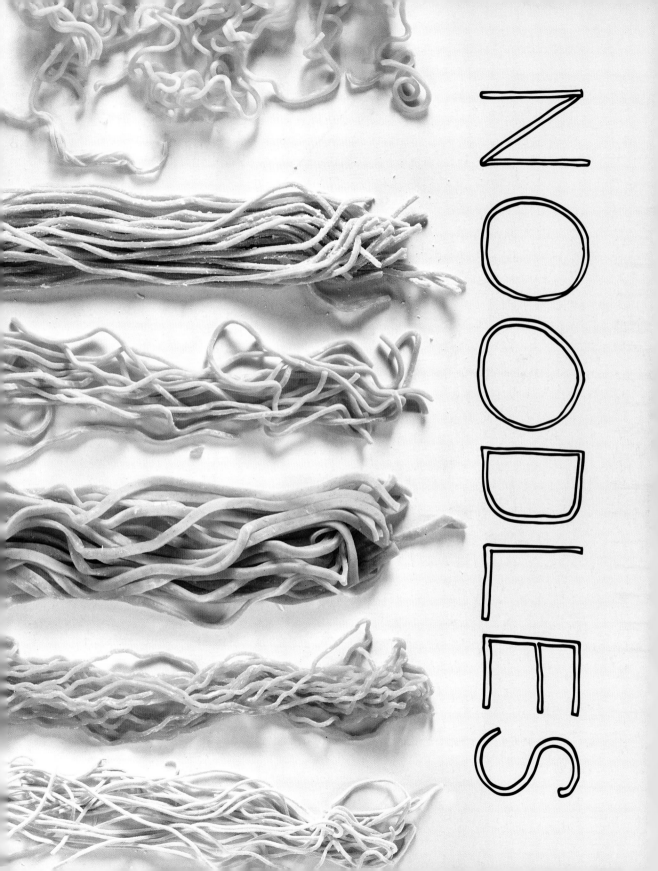

NOODLES

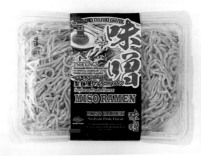

MISO / THICKER NOODLE / WAVY OR STRAIGHT / HARD CHEW

A thick, rich miso ramen calls for a thicker noodle, which, yes, goes against my earlier "thicker soup, thinner noodle" concept—but that's my preference and the way I ate my first life-changing bowl of miso ramen years ago. When a miso soup is emulsified, the fat and miso just hug a thicker noodle and you have a really hearty bowl. Now, converse to that, we make a lighter-style spicy miso at the shop that takes a thinner noodle.

A great bowl of ramen takes experimentation, and the only way to get there is to test different types of noodles.

Noodles to Buy

FROZEN/FRESH

This is the ideal product, and if you live in a city with a decent Japanese market, you will most likely be able to find frozen/fresh ramen noodles. Do not be put off by frozen. The freezing actually preserves the noodle really well.

A note about fake ramen noodles . . . There are some high-end grocery stores that have caught on to the ramen craze and are selling what they call ramen. Poppycock! Don't fall for it. Bypass them and go straight to the Japanese or Asian market.

DRIED

There is nothing wrong with dried noodles, but you likely won't find actual, true dried ramen noodles.

Second to ramen noodles, I would use white soba or somen. White soba is a wheat noodle without the kansui, or alkaline—it just won't have the same bite, and it is my go-to everyday noodle in the house. You will find a lot of dried noodles at the market. Just stay away from anything that says "egg noodle;" it will be too soft and will dissipate too fast.

Cooking Noodles

Cook noodles according to the package, as they all vary. But if you're using frozen ramen noodles, thaw them, then boil them in a large pot of unseasoned boiling water. Stir the noodles occasionally to ensure that they cook evenly and to untangle the strands. Ramen noodles don't like being in the cold air after they have begun to cook, so if you are either batch cooking for all your bowls or cooking your noodles in individual baskets, you will want to gently place them in your ramen bowls with broth as quickly as possible. I will cover this again in Ramen Bowl Assembly (see page 154).

Kenshiro Uki (Sun Noodle)

\\\\\

You literally grew up with ramen. Tell me what role eating ramen played in your life growing up in the ramen noodle business?

It literally sums up my memories as a child. Every Sunday, our family would go and visit a ramen shop to enjoy the newest bowl my dad wanted to try. My sister and I were the taste testers for anything Sun Noodle was thinking of launching on the retail store shelves. They believed that if kids liked it, parents would buy it. We were R&Ders from a young age. Every night, our parents would bring home a different type of noodle, a different type of soup base. Many of the products still on the store shelves today are the ones my sister and I approved.

What's the first style of ramen you can remember and is it your favorite go-to style?

Hawaii was filled with ramen shops focusing on miso and shoyu, so that's what I grew up eating. Miso ramen is still my go-to ramen. I enjoy the Sapporo-style miso ramen where everything is made in a wok, one bowl at a time. The broth is rich, noodles are chewy, and the butter-and-corn combo is what I still crave every day.

Tell us simply: What is the main difference between pasta and a ramen noodle?

Pasta is made with durum semolina flour, water, and sometimes egg. Durum is a type of wheat that has a very high protein percentage. Ramen, on the other hand, is usually made with medium protein flour, water, salt, and kansui (potassium carbonate, sodium carbonate). It's actually a rule in the industry in Japan that if there is no kansui, it cannot officially be called a ramen noodle. Kansui brings out the alkaline aroma in the noodle and also helps with the development of gluten.

What is the process for choosing the proper noodle for a specific style of ramen?

A bowl of ramen is all about balance. However, the noodles and broth need to match. Rule of thumb is that one should not overpower the other. You can have a great noodle, but if it doesn't match the soup, it doesn't result in a great bowl of ramen. The basic is that the thicker the broth, the thicker the noodle should be and heartier, and I tend to agree. When I sit down to a bowl of thick miso I want a hearty noodle. My Tonkotsu is rather light— so we chose a thinner noodle. Balance, that's pretty much it.

What is your favorite thing about the U.S. ramen market? So many people identify ramen as only Japanese—how is ramen becoming American?

The U.S. ramen market is probably one of the more exciting markets because we have a lot of talented chefs from different culinary backgrounds who are experimenting with ramen. We have people who are not afraid to challenge and think outside of the box. I think it's always important to respect the fundamentals, but it's also just as important to innovate. We see that happening here in the U.S.

What would you say are the greatest differences in flavor and execution between American and Japanese ramen?

This is hard to say, especially today, since there are a lot of ramen shops opening around Japan experimenting with flavors that would be considered nontraditional. However, if there is a common comment within the industry, I often hear that Japanese ramen is not as bold or salty as ramen found in the U.S.

What do you think is the greatest misconception about ramen noodles and ramen in general?

That [it] should be cheap. Yes, it's an affordable meal, but the amount of ingredients, labor, and work it takes to make a consistently good bowl of ramen is very challenging. Talented chefs work hard to get this done and spend many hours preparing and perfecting their bowl of ramen. In my mind, we should be able to appreciate and pay fifteen dollars for a bowl of ramen just like we would do for a plate of Italian pasta.

What's the ramen secret you wish everyone could know?

The perception that Japanese flour is top quality is a myth. The wheat found in most ramen manufacturers in Japan is from Canada, U.S., and Australia. The milling companies in Japan have [the technology that enables them] to finely mill the flour.

What advice do you have for someone trying to make ramen noodles from scratch?

For people making ramen from home, it's always great to experiment with wheat sourced from different parts of the world. The wheat and how the wheat is milled into flour will result in very different noodles. Temperature and humidity control are very important as they will have a direct effect on how the noodles come out.

Where in the U.S. do you see the most exciting ramen being created?

Most exciting? New York. Fastest-growing market would be Texas.

What's the most extreme interpretation of ramen that you have eaten? Can it go too far and break too many rules?

Truffle ramen blended with cheese and miso. It was good, but I don't think I would want to eat it every day.

THE BIRTH OF NASHVILLE'S XL RAMEN FESTIVAL

While I was still running Otaku as a pop-up, there came a point when I was getting one or two calls a week to do pop-ups at different locations and restaurants. It was a PR machine and it was a novelty, as no one had done anything like this in Nashville before. One of these calls was from the owner of a 15,000-square-foot music venue. He asked, "I have a friend who owns a catering company that services concert tours and has a warehouse full of kitchen equipment, do you want to do a pop-up here?" I was serving a maximum of two hundred bowls at the time, but I said, "Hell yeah, let's do this!" and foolishly and fearlessly I charged into that opportunity.

Thus, the premier Extra Large Ramen Festival was kicked off in 2013 at Marathon Music Works. That first year it was indoors and we used induction burners to heat our water and stocks (which never quite put out the level of heat you want)—it was really insane. But we sold one thousand bowls of ramen and had a great time.

The next year rolled around and by then I was starting to build my relationships in the ramen world and have access to more talent. So I had a phone call with Kenshiro, who graciously supported the event through Sun Noodle, to figure out who to invite. We ended

up with ramen royalty in the form of Ivan Orkin (Ivan Ramen, Slurp Shop), Yuji Haraguchi (Okonomi, Yuji Ramen), Shigetoshi "Jack" Nakamura aka Naka (Ramen Lab), Jessica Benefield (Two Ten Jack, Nashville), and my shop Otaku Ramen. An all-star cast.

It all happened in February and, as luck would have it, coincided with a huge storm in New York. We had presold every single bowl, and all our talent . . . was stuck in New York. Flights kept getting canceled, and I was up for twenty-four hours trying to rebook for these guys. By five a.m., I was on the phone for the fiftieth time with Kenshiro and he said, "All right, I am going to go rent an SUV, pick everybody up, and drive them to Nashville." I thought, Kenshiro, you are a hero among men.

So he called Yuji and Naka and I said I'd call Ivan to tell him the deal. Ivan said, "Drive? No, no, my flight hasn't been canceled, I'll call you back." *Click.* I didn't hear from him for two hours, and when I did, he was at the airport. His flight was the only one to make it out of JFK. He arrived first, at about ten a.m., and I picked him up. Here I was in my car with Ivan, very intimidated (watch his *Chef's Table* episode and you will feel me), and no doubt annoying the hell out of him with my chitter-chatter. I took Ivan over to the kitchen and we hung out while he did his prep, then I took him around Nashville and showed him the town. No doubt the South was a foreign land to him, a good New York Jew in Nashville. But as I took him to all my regular haunts, Southern hospitality began to completely disarm him and his regular kvetching started to melt away.

It was wonderful, I had him nice and pliable when we got back to the kitchen and I thought, *This is my moment I gotta do it . . . I have to feed him my bowl of ramen and get his feedback.* I was scared to death. As I was cooking, he started to ask me questions like, "Where do you get your chickens?" and I didn't have any answers. Finally he said, "Stop, just stop. Because you don't

continues >

have to know the answers to these questions, but if you want to be good at this, then you need to." I literally almost started crying. It was an unusual place to be in because I didn't work for him but I obviously looked up to him. He is a father figure in the ramen industry, not only because of his age but because it's the role he plays. I don't know the Japanese culture as well as I look forward to knowing it as the years go on, but I know that he is very Japanese—strong and demonstrative.

That moment was a turning point for me and made me rethink everything I did—*What am I doing? What do I care about and what do I stand for?*—instead of just go, go, go. When I was a rep, agent, and salesperson in the entertainment industry, I was basically trained to be Sisyphus. I would push that boulder up that hill every day for my clients, it would smack me in the face, and I would smile and get up and do it again. I loved the struggle and the strife, and learned to manage that. But the ball was so far out in front of me at this point, I could barely keep up with the ramen shop, the pop-up, and the ramen fest, in the BEST way possible. I felt

like every day I woke up I'd ask the universe for something and it would appear, literally. It had never been more apparent that I should be doing this, but it was so much. I do ask myself a lot, *Why is this happening to me?* When you've worked so hard to go after this idea of success and then your passion becomes your job, it's really a unique thing. People ask me why ramen is important, and I have a hard time responding without waxing poetic. Those of us who do it aren't trying to conquer the world; we do it because we love it. A good bowl of ramen makes people happy. When I see people sitting in my shop eating noodles, kids giggling and happy, it melts me.

Finally the boys pulled up in the SUV, we unloaded as fast as we could, the beer and sake was served, and it was all Japanese from there on out. It was unbelievable to stand there with so many people I admired, in my kitchen. Another fun thing about it was how easy it was to get so many talented cooks to volunteer at the event. Every chef in Nashville wanted to be in this kitchen. We sold three thousand bowls of ramen the next day for my favorite charity, Pablove, which funds grants for pediatric cancer. Of course, Ivan being Ivan, he was the first one to eighty-six and run out of bowls. It was extraordinary.

After it was all done, I took all the chefs for a drive in the country. I didn't understand a single thing they said in Japanese in the car, but I could hear the wonderment in their voices and in their questions. It was a beautiful winter day. I took them to a little town called Leiper's Fork, and they poked around antique stores. People stared at them, not understanding why there were all these young Japanese men wandering through. Now, it's actually not that unusual in Nashville because we have Nissan and Bridgestone headquartered here, but they loved it. We had a big bonfire outside, and by the end of the day my face literally hurt from smiling so much. Who knows who will be at the next XL Ramen Festival?

Shigetoshi Nakamura (Nakamura NYC)

\\\

Tell me what role eating ramen played in your life growing up in Japan.

Ramen as a dish is like my first love, from the moment I ate it. When I became an elementary school student, I had instant noodles for the first time and it was quite a shock. Because when I was introduced to ramen, I had been taught how to enjoy food in all its beauty: the appearance of the noodles, the taste and fragrance of the soup and its toppings.

What's the first style of ramen you can remember and is it your favorite go-to style?

I do not know if this should be called a style, but I preferred eating chicken broth soy sauce instant noodles. Handmade noodles are only available in noodle shops, and handmade noodles for me at a young age were like a reward once a month. However, the instant noodles with chicken broth soy sauce, which I ate on a daily basis, is the foundation of my ramen now.

You have taught me a lot about styles of ramen. What are your favorite Japanese styles of ramen that you wish ramen shops would serve in the U.S.?

In Japan, various ramen shops of various styles were born with various excellent ingredients, but in the American market there are not yet as many variations as in Japan. But when you look at instant noodles sold at the grocery store in the United States, there are all sorts of kinds that cannot be defeated by Japan, and they are also a taste and style not found in Japan. From that point of view, I hope that ramen will continue to evolve into the future, and will incorporate the unique food culture of the United States.

What is the difference between iekei-style and tonkotsu shoyu?

Essentially, iekei and tonkotsu shoyu ramen are very similar because of the pork broth and shoyu tare. However, iekei ramen usually has more chicken broth mixed in volume-wise than tonkotsu shoyu. Also, iekei has very consistent toppings that are simple and include roasted pork, spinach, and seaweed.

What is your "style"?

My style is chicken broth soy sauce ramen. It is the most orthodox style in the Kanto, with fine noodles in a crystal-clear chicken broth.

You have made ramen on the West Coast and the East Coast, as well as in Japan. What is your favorite thing about the U.S. ramen market? So many people identify ramen as only Japanese; how is ramen becoming American?

People think that ramen food culture is due to the influence of land and climate in Japan. Japanese people like long noodles, and it seems that various noodle dishes have been transmitted from China, but thin and long ramen has particularly evolved among them. And, in the process of its evolution, I think that Japan's unique ramen was born while being influenced by Japanese food culture. I think that ramen will also evolve while incorporating the trends in food culture, the way rolled sushi has evolved in America.

What would you say are the greatest differences in flavor and execution between American and Japanese ramen?

In Japan, I was preparing ramen while feeling the balance as ramen is important, but in America I try to make ramen, which is extremely easy to understand, by specializing in something (hotness and thickness).

What's the ramen secret you wish everyone could know?

It is said that the taste changes according to the number of noodles you eat in a bite. Please try it.

Where in the U.S. do you see the most exciting ramen being created?

Although I do not know too many ramen shops outside of my own, I am very fascinated with ramen styles unique to a certain region and a certain season.

There is simply nothing more nourishing and satisfying than a bowl of soup. Bone broth itself has not only become the darling of the wellness world, but it has garnered bragging rights for chefs and cooks worldwide for centuries. As long as there have been chicken bones, pork bones, beef bones, and water, there has been stock.

For an American girl like me, my mom's chicken noodle soup was magic because it always made me feel better. Moms do that, but it was something else: the stock. Looking back, with my knowledge of stock today, I know why. That lick-your-lips thickness to a great bowl of chicken soup is created by the presence of fat and collagen. They're vital players in a ramen bowl, and your aim when making ramen broth is to extract ALL the goodness of the bones into the water.

One of the things I learned quickly is that making ramen stock is the total inverse of making a stock using the French method. For ramen, I was taught to use only bones and water. Do not use mirepoix (vegetables) and seasonings, because they change the broth's color and viscosity. The tare, oil, and topping do the flavor work. A ramen stock also has a higher ratio of bones to water than a traditional broth. When you taste your completed ramen stock, you should taste the very essence of the chicken and bones.

The stock is the canvas on which you will create your ramen bowl.

Stock versus Broth

What's the difference? This is a topic of much debate. But I will simplify for our purposes.

Broth can have vegetables, aromatics, meat, and bones. It has a shorter cooking time and is seasoned. Stock has a longer cooking time and is unseasoned.

Broth is typically used as a soup base, whereas stock is used more for its viscosity, gelatin, and collagen, as well as minerals.

Enter bone broth (I know, it's confusing).

BONE BROTH

You got it, bone broth is a stock made from bones, water, and vegetables, cooked at a lower heat for a longer period to extract the minerals and collagen (gelatin), and then seasoned like a broth. It's the best of both worlds. Everyone seems to be obsessed with making it or buying it, and with good reason. It's really, really good for you when you use the bones of responsibly raised animals. It promotes fast-growing nails and hair; plump, glowing skin; and a host of positive internal side effects.

But I have to tell you, many of the bone broths I see on the market make me scratch my head because they don't contain any fat—and the fat is the key.

Now, let's get nerdy for a minute about the actual wellness power of a well-made bone broth. The minerals you extract from the bones are calcium and magnesium, which promote a healthy gut and strong bones. The collagen and fat act as escorts for those minerals to promote an anti-inflammatory benefit for humans (and many animals), but the key here is the relationship of the collagen and fat to the equation. So don't skimp, either in a simple broth or in a ramen broth. Those two elements are vital, and with time, if you make and drink these broths often, you will see the lovely cosmetic effects in your nails, hair, and skin. (Seriously, this happens.)

Now you can rejoice because I have just told you that ramen is good for you—and it's true. We are beginning to unravel some of the mystery about exactly why ramen makes you so happy. It's still magic, but now we have a little science to back it up.

THE KEY TO BONE BROTH

Bone broth is only as good as its bones and water.

Water

I always try to use the cleanest water I can: filtered, mineral, spring, or reverse osmosis (the gold standard). If you begin with great-tasting water, you'll have great-tasting broth. Simple.

Bones

Use the highest-quality animal you can get. Organic, natural, grass fed, it's your choice. You are extracting everything from these bones, and I know I don't want to ingest hormones, so spend the extra money and get the best bones and meat you can find. Fat hens work best for making ramen stock because the meat adds flavor and the bones are nice and big, so ask your butcher if they can get you a hen. You will probably have good luck at your farmers market as well. Use skin-on always, to get all that beautiful chicken fat.

The recipes will highlight the specific bones that are best to use in each recipe.

Some ramen shops like to make combo broths, chicken and pork bones together for example, but I am a purist, and we make singular stocks at the shop and combine on order. One of the simplest reasons for making singular stocks is that sometimes you may want to make a big batch of broth and use it for another soup or as a stock for cooking. Another reason is because it's more precise when creating your own flavors if, for example, you can note a recipe should have ¼ beef stock + ¼ chicken stock + ½ pork stock. Making adjustments to your broth is much easier this way, and you can never have too much stock in your freezer.

COOKING BONE BROTH

Let's talk about your stove. What kind of heat will you be using? The answer will affect the style you choose to make your stock.

Stovetops

The most common method is going to take a lot of time and attention, but it's worth it.

Gas. This is the most widely used and loved stovetop heat source. The only hindrance is that these broths can take up to twelve hours to complete, and it's not wise to leave a pot on a gas stove overnight. (In other words, don't do it. I almost burned my house down talking myself into thinking this would be okay.) So it's going to be an early morning (for a few days in a row) to complete your stock if you go this route.

Electric or induction. Both are safe and steady. The heat is controlled and consistent and allows you to safely cook a stock for a long time, even unattended overnight.

Pressure cooking. Cooking with pressure has a handful of pretty convincing upsides. When it comes to making ramen stock, it both reduces cooking time by close to three ve and removes oxygen from the process. The result is a vibrant stock made with no mess in a fraction of the time. No-brainer. But (there is always a but) it could be argued that the downside is the liquid simply doesn't have as long to impart the flavors you are asking it to with a shorter cook time. And as much as I love the speed and efficiency of the pressure cooker broth method, there's really nothing quite like hunkering down in the winter and spending a full day tending to stock on the stovetop, preferably while bingeing on Netflix. The stovetop stock method is the one you'll want to use for those days, and it will make your house smell absolutely incredible. But many of you will opt for the pressure cooker because of the realities of time and life. The old-school pot on the stovetop will do the trick, but if you have not already caught on to the Instant Pot craze, now is the time. I seriously cannot live without mine.

THE WORLD-FAMOUS PAITAN IN GINZA

On our last trip to Japan, my husband and I stood in line for an hour and a half for a bowl of ramen. Not just any bowl—a bowl of tori paitan that was a bowl of legends. The shop had just eight seats and was very small on the inside . . . and the bowl was the most beautiful I had ever seen. The bright yellow, milky broth smelled like pure chicken. The texture . . . Oh my goodness, the texture: silky with just the right amount of fat. There was no oil floating on the top of this ramen (as in shio or shoyu), because it was emulsified. I did not hear hand blenders whirring in this shop. Not even so much as a whisk—simply the quiet ladling of this magical soup.

A few days later I was following my friends Brian (Ramen Adventures) and Hiroshi (Ramen Beast) around to eat some ramen and we got to talking about this particular shop. I began to calculate: "I was there for an hour and a half and I saw at least twenty-five to thirty people per hour get served. Multiply that by the six hours they are open and I'm going to guess these guys are pushing two hundred bowls a day. At twelve ounces of stock per bowl, that is close to twenty gallons a day of soup. Hmmm, how do I say this . . . There is NO WAY these guys are making that much stock in that tiny shop. So it's being made somewhere else." Somehow the thought that a chef makes and serves all his ramen out of one tiny shop makes them feel like, well, masters.

That thought lingered in the taxicab for a minute; that this legendary and delicious soup was made somewhere else changed our overall perception. I was also now certain emulsification played a big role. They were using a hand blender, or a blender of some sort, the same way we were to create that texture for the soup. You, too, can make a silky paitan with a great stock and emulsification.

CHINTAN (清湯) "CLEAR SOUP"

Since the late 1800s, when the Chinese began immigrating to Japan, many Chinese words have been adopted into the ramen lexicon. *Chintan* is the word we ramen-making folks use to describe a clear soup, no matter what type of bone it is made with. The most common is a *tori chintan*, or chicken soup. If this is the point where you say to yourself, *Oh yeah, I know how to make chicken stock*, I'll just skip ahead, stop yourself and keep reading. I have taught dozens of French-trained chefs how to make this stock, and the response is always the same: "I had no idea." I will dare to say that you have most likely been making burned chicken stock your whole life and you never knew.

Timing-wise, ideally you want to start the chintan in the morning so you can have time to make paitan (page 88) on the same day, but you can hold the bones overnight in the fridge and start the paitan the following day, if necessary.

2 pounds chicken feet

1 (5-to-6-pound) whole chicken

8 cups water (or a 2:1 water-to-bones ratio, using volume)

2 cups thinly sliced skin-on ginger

1 (12 x 12-inch) piece kombu

TORI CHINTAN

// MAKES ABOUT 6 CUPS

All chicken, clear stock.

TO PREPARE

1 Blanch the chicken feet: In a large, heavy-bottomed stockpot, arrange the feet and add enough cool water to just cover. Bring to a boil over high heat. As soon as the water reaches a boil, remove from the heat and dump out the water.

2 Cut the chicken: With the tip of a sharp knife, cut the wings off and place them in a stockpot or pressure cooker vessel. Remove the breast meat by guiding your knife along both sides of the cartilage at the end of the breastbone. Reserve the breast meat for

recipe continues >

another use (such as the toppings in the Lemon Chicken Paitan, page 181). Turn the chicken breast side down. Cut lengthwise down the center of the chicken, separating the thighs, to split the chicken into quarters.

3   Tightly pack the chicken parts, including the skin and bones, into the pot. The goal here is for the bones to remain relatively still while they cook, not roll around. Arrange the blanched feet in a tight formation on top of the chicken. If you have the space in your fridge, place the whole pot in there to chill for 1 hour. Why? To let those chicken feet gel together and form a sort of raft on top of the bones. The raft will float on the whole surface of the pot. If you simply don't have the space in your fridge to do this, just watch your stock carefully as it comes up to temp to ensure that it never boils. This will allow the feet to leach the collagen to seal the pot, which will keep oxygen out. The lack of oxygen is the key to a beautiful golden stock.

4   Remove the pot or vessel from the fridge and fill it with just enough water to cover, about 8 cups—the ideal ratio is 2:1 water to bones; you don't want to drown them.

STOVETOP METHOD

1   This is the most common method for making stock and can have incredible results, but you must keep a close eye to ensure you do not burn the stock, which is very easy to do. If the heat reaches 200°F or higher too fast, your stock will burn and smell faintly of rubber tires. Your goal is to raise the heat slowly and maintain a slow, steady simmer, which will yield a rich, clean stock. Use your temperature gauge on the pot to keep a watch on it.

2   Affix the temperature gauge to the side of the pot and heat to medium. You do not want to see bubbles or steam coming off the pot, or bones rolling around. You are looking for molten stillness. Bring the broth to 190 to 200°F. Don't rush this process; it should take about an hour to get the pot to the right temperature. In raising the temperature slowly, you will see the chicken feet begin to release the fat, which will eventually "seal" the pot, trapping in oxygen and steam. Reduce the temperature to 190°F and you should see what we call a low bubble, or a few bubbles but not a boil. A filmy brown foam will begin to rise to the top at this point—ignore it. Don't skim the stock. Trust me, you want the foam. It has essential amino acids in it, plus it acts as a raft to help clarify the stock for the next 30 to 45 minutes. When you

recipe continues >

start to see a layer of the fat coming off the bones and feet, cover the pot to keep oxygen out (oxygen will oxidize your stock, giving it an unappealing dingy color).

3   Continue simmering at a low bubble of 180 to 190°F for 6 hours. No stirring, ever.

4   While the broth is cooking, prepare a large bowl or container (or several smaller bowls/containers) to chill the broth in, and clear space in your refrigerator.

5   When the broth has reached a rich golden color, your entire house will smell like incredible chicken soup. At this point, when you (carefully) taste the hot broth, it should have a lick-your-lips, pure-chicken quality (or it should read 4 to 5 Brix on a refractometer, if you have one). It should taste of chicken first, not water. If your stock tastes like water first, give it another hour at 200 to 210°F to reduce a little. Don't let this stock cook longer than 6 hours or it will begin to reduce, lose its clarity, and the color will become less vibrant.

6   Strain your stock into the prepared bowl or container, and then add the ginger and kombu. Reserve the bones for tori paitan broth. Allow the ingredients to steep in the broth for about 40 minutes at room temperature, then strain the

ginger and kombu out and discard. Cover the broth and chill in the refrigerator until it is totally solid and gelatinous, a minimum of 3 to 4 hours or overnight.

7   When the broth is totally chilled and a thick layer of fat has formed on top, use a spoon to skim off the fat and reserve it for making Infused Chicken Fat (page 102).

8   The chintan will last 1 week in the refrigerator or 2 months in the freezer.

PRESSURE COOKER METHOD

1   Grab your packed vessel from the fridge and add enough water to cover. Lock the top and set your cooker on high pressure for 90 minutes. The stock will reach just around 210°F and the high pressure will move the process along three times faster than the stovetop method. Remember to allow the steam to release naturally, instead of forcing it (which will bring the broth to a rapid boil and disturb the clarity). When the steam has fully dissipated, the top lock will release so you can open and behold your beautiful golden stock.

2   While the broth is cooking, prepare a large bowl or container (or several smaller bowls/containers) to chill the broth in, and clear space in your refrigerator.

3   Carefully taste the broth. It should have a lick-your-lips, pure-chicken quality (or read 4 to 5 Brix on a refractometer, if you have one). Your chicken stock should have a golden clear color and should taste of chicken first, not water. If your stock is too light, strain the bones out, place the stock back in the pot, set the open cooker to sauté and allow the stock to reduce for no more than 20 minutes.

4   Strain your stock into the prepared bowl or container and then add the ginger and kombu. Reserve bones for the Tori Paitan. Allow the ingredients to steep in the broth for about 40 minutes at room temperature, then strain the ginger and kombu out and discard. Cover the broth and chill in the refrigerator until it is totally solid and gelatinous, a minimum of 3 to 4 hours or overnight.

5   When the broth is totally chilled and a thick layer of fat has formed on top, use a spoon to skim off the fat and reserve it for making Infused Chicken Fat (page 102).

6   The chintan will keep for 1 week in the refrigerator or 2 months in the freezer.

Stockpot Note

If using the stovetop method, use a large (8- to 12-quart) stockpot with a heavy bottom, if possible—the taller and skinnier it is, the better, as it limits the broth's exposure to air and helps create a delicious fat seal on top.

Chicken Bones Note

Use organic hens if possible, as they are more plump and have more delicious fat. Chicken feet can be procured at many butchers and Asian groceries. You can have your butcher quarter your chicken for you, but be sure they give you the whole bird. You want the spine and skin as well, as they add flavor and collagen to the broth. Finally, don't be afraid of blood; it helps clarify the stock and makes it sweet. If you see it in the bones or carcass, it's okay!

PAITAN (白湯) "WHITE SOUP"

The first time I had a tori paitan was at Totto Ramen in NYC. I sat in amazement and just kept asking myself, This is just chicken broth? What I didn't understand was how it could be creamy like that . . . without cream. I was so mesmerized by it that I set out to learn how to make it. I had never had a creamy chicken broth until I had ramen, even though I grew up eating a lot of chicken soup in the South. My mom excels at it, and sometimes she'd make a creamy chicken soup, but it was usually canned, or she used dairy to thicken it. The fact that you could extract the marrow from chicken bones to make it a creamy broth was mind-blowing to me.

Tonkotsu, the milky-white pork broth and arguably the world's most popular ramen broth and style, is also technically a paitan, as it is a cloudy stock and the name of the game is extracting the marrow to give it the milky-white look and texture.

Another valuable piece of the paitan puzzle to note here is emulsification. You want to basically blend your strained stock either in a blender like a Vitamix or with an immersion hand blender, which I prefer because it creates less mess. Emulsifying, or blending, makes the larger fat globules into smaller globules and is the key to a great tori paitan or tonkotsu. When I started making ramen, I knew enough to know that all those pretty little balls of oil floating in the bowl when I took a sip made the whole bowl better, but admittedly it took me a while to figure out that you had to emulsify to get the creamy texture. So if you are going to get serious about making these broths, buy a handheld immersion blender. (Not expensive.)

1 recipe Tori Chintan
(page 82)

TORI PAITAN

// MAKES ABOUT 5 CUPS

This stock is a two-step process. The first step is making a chintan with either the stovetop or pressure cooker method.

recipe continues >

STOVETOP METHOD

1 After making and straining off your chintan, add water to the bones and crank up the heat to high. The stock will come to a boil. You want the bones to roll and come apart, releasing everything left in them. Boil on high for about 1 hour and 30 minutes, until the bones look depleted (there should be no soft tissue or cartilage left; everything should have melted into the soup) and you have a milky-white stock. Your refractometer should read 7 to 9 Brix for a thick, rich paitan, or have the consistency of a light gravy.

2 When the broth is complete, pull some of the largest and cleanest bones out to make room for your hand blender. Using a hand blender, carefully agitate the stock to release any extra bits of marrow and emulsify them into the liquid.

3 Carefully strain the soup into a large bowl or container, discarding the bones. Cover the broth and chill in the refrigerator until it is totally solid and gelatinous, a minimum of 3 to 4 hours or overnight. (There is no need to skim the paitan.)

4 The paitan will keep for 3 days in the refrigerator or 2 months in the freezer.

PRESSURE COOKER METHOD

1 Once your pressure cooker beeps and lets you know your chintan is complete, you can force the steam valve to release, which will raise the temperature inside the vessel and bring the stock to a boil. Once you're able to open the cooker, set it to the highest sauté or boil setting it will allow to keep the stock at a rolling boil until it begins to look milky white and has the consistency of a light gravy, about 1 hour and 30 minutes.

2 When the broth is complete, pull some of the largest and cleanest bones out to make room for your hand blender. Using a hand blender, carefully agitate the stock to release any extra bits of marrow and emulsify them into the liquid.

3 Carefully strain the soup into a large bowl or container, discarding the bones. Cover the broth and chill in the refrigerator until it is totally solid and gelatinous, a minimum of 3 to 4 hours or overnight. (There is no need to skim the paitan.)

4 The paitan will keep for 3 days in the refrigerator or 2 months in the freezer.

3 pounds pork femurs, cut into 2-inch pieces (so you can look through the center of the bone and see the marrow)

2 pounds pork neck (or any other main scrap)

1 trotter

10 to 12 cups water (or 2:1 water-to-bones ratio using volume)

Two 12 x 12-inch pieces kombu

TONKOTSU (豚骨) "PORK BONE"

// MAKES ABOUT 8 CUPS

This is the mother of ramen stock. It has a concentrated and deep flavor that is not for the faint of heart. It's porky and fatty to the core, and it's an insanely rewarding stock to make. I used to sit for hours waiting for that marrow cloud to rise up through the liquid. Even to this day, every single time I see it, I clench my fists above my head in victory. This famed cloudy pork bone stock is, again, simply bones and water, but the process to get what you want out of these bones takes patience.

In a large stockpot, place the bones and add water to cover. Bring to a boil over high heat and blanch the bones for 10 minutes. Drain the pot, let the bones cool, then run each bone under cold water, cleaning off the scum with your hands. Clean off as much dirt and impurities from the bones as you can.

Once cleaned, allow the bones to rest in the fridge for 2 to 3 hours to allow the marrow to come off the bone a bit and slide right out in the next phase of making our stock. (Meanwhile, wash your stockpot if using the stovetop method.)

STOVETOP METHOD

1 Begin with a clean stockpot and your congealed bones. Add a 2:1 ratio of water to bones, or just enough water to cover (10 to 12 cups). You don't want to drown them, but make sure they have enough room to roll in the moving pot. Affix your temperature gauge to the pot. Bring the stock to a boil (220°F) over high heat (it will take about 30 minutes). Once the stock reaches a rolling boil, reduce the heat to medium (190°F). If a filmy brown foam begins to rise to the top at this point, skim off as much as possible until there is no more.

recipe continues >

2 Continue cooking at a medium boil for at least 6 hours (you can go as long as 8), then raise the heat to a hard boil. Slowly add water to keep the water level the same. Boil and agitate the bones until you see that marrow cloud and all the cartilage and soft tissue on the bones has literally melted into the stock. The bones should look like dinosaur bones when you pull them out, even with a slight chalkiness from the calcium leached from them.

3 While the broth is cooking, prepare a large glass or food-grade plastic bowl or container (Tupperware will melt; don't use it here) to chill the broth in, and clear space in your refrigerator.

4 When the broth is complete, pull some of the largest and cleanest bones out to make room for your hand blender. Using a hand blender, carefully agitate the stock to release any extra bits of marrow and emulsify them into the liquid.

5 Strain your stock into the prepared bowl or container and then add the kombu. Allow it to steep in the broth for about 50 minutes at room temperature, then strain out and discard. Cover the broth and chill in the refrigerator until it is totally solid and gelatinous, a minimum of 3 to 4 hours or overnight.

6 When the broth is totally chilled and a thick layer of fat has formed on top, use a spoon to skim off the fat and reserve it for making Infused Pork Fat (page 105).

7 The tonkotsu will keep for 1 week in the refrigerator or 2 months in the freezer.

PRESSURE COOKER METHOD

1 Add the cleaned bones to the pressure cooker vessel, then add water using a 2:1 water-to-bones ratio (10 to 12 cups). Lock the top and set your cooker to high for 2 hours. Force the steam valve to release, which will bring the temperature of the stock up and force a boil.

2 When the top unlocks, unplug the cooker and allow the stock to rest for 1 hour, then return to a hard boil either on high in the cooker itself, or transfer it all to a stockpot and boil over high heat for 1 to 2 hours, or until the stock looks milky and cloudy. This means the marrow has come out of the bones.

3 At this point, inspect your stock. You're looking for a few things: The stock should be opaque from the marrow of the bones, and there should be no soft tissue or cartilage left on the bones. The bones will appear chalky from decalcification. If the stock needs to cook longer, put it back on for another 30 minutes on high.

4   When the broth is complete, pull some of the largest and cleanest bones out to make room for your hand blender. Using a hand blender, carefully agitate the stock to release any extra bits of marrow and emulsify them into the liquid. For the last hour add the kombu and allow the essential glutamates to leach out and give your stock all the umami you are looking for.

5   Strain the stock into a large glass or food-grade plastic bowl or container (I do not recommend your typical plastic container; this stock will melt your Tupperware). Cover the broth and chill in the refrigerator until it is totally solid and gelatinous, a minimum of 3 to 4 hours or overnight.

6   When the broth is totally chilled and a thick layer of fat has formed on top, use a spoon to skim off the fat and reserve it for making Infused Pork Fat (page 105).

7   The tonkotsu will keep for 1 week in the refrigerator or 2 months in the freezer.

Pork Bones Note

Use organic and all-natural pork if possible. I bet your butcher at the market will be thrilled to sell you those bones. Ask them to cut your femur bones for you, too.

Stockpot Note

If using the stovetop method, use a large (8- to 12-quart) stockpot with a heavy bottom, if possible—the taller and skinnier it is, the better, as it limits the broth's exposure to air and helps create a delicious fat seal on top.

Pro Tip

Once it's finished cooking, it's very important to cool a pork broth down quickly. I usually set up an ice bath in my sink for the stockpot or vessel and stir occasionally to continue the cooling process. If you live where the snow flies, use nature and cool your stockpot outside.

3 cups filtered water, at room temperature

One ½-ounce piece kombu

1 cup niboshi (dried anchovies)

1 cup katsuobushi (dried bonito flakes)

2 awase dashi packets

COLD-BREWED DASHI

// MAKES 2 CUPS

Dashi is one of the foundations of Japanese cuisine. This simple combination of kombu and bonito flakes steeped together creates a broth high in naturally occurring glutamine, which lends umami and a lick-your-lips viscosity to countless dishes, which is a very Japanese flavor profile. In ramen, dashi is rarely used as a broth on its own (eaten plain, it doesn't taste like much), but combined with other broths and seasonings, it makes everything come together in an almost magical way.

I like this cold-steeping method for making dashi because it creates a more intense flavor and viscosity. It takes longer (two days), but the time spent is largely inactive, so I think it's worth it. Since dashi is rarely used on its own, it's easy to double should you want to make more. Dashi can be used to add flavor to virtually anything in lieu of water. Dashi is the secret to great miso soup, dashimaki omelets, and so much more.

You can make a quicker version of dashi with just the awase dashi packets, which are available online or in Asian grocery stores.

For more on these ingredients, see the "Pantry" section (page 39).

1 Use a damp towel to wipe off the white substance on the outside of the kombu, but do not run it under water. This powdery white substance will add a metallic taste to the dashi if not properly cleaned.

2 Remove the heads of the niboshi for the same reason (I just pop them off with my fingers and discard).

3 Stir the kombu, niboshi, katsuobushi, and awase dashi packets into the water and allow to soak in the refrigerator for 48 hours covered.

4 Strain the liquid and discard all solids. The dashi will keep for up to 4 days, tightly covered, in the refrigerator.

3 corncobs

1 pound Idaho potatoes,
  peeled and chopped

4 stalks celery, chopped

1 medium onion, chopped

3 medium carrots, chopped

¼ cup black peppercorns

10 cups water

VEGETABLE STOCK

// MAKES ABOUT 6 CUPS

For a ramen chef, this stock is always, well, the stock that we continue to try to improve. It will never match the unctuousness of a bone broth, so what we are going for here is flavor and balance. This is a light stock that can easily take the saltiness of a shoyu tare or the creaminess of a miso tare. In other words, it's versatile. Think of your veg stock a little bit like freeform jazz. Use what you have, make notes, and adjust the seasoning as your palate tells you.

STOVETOP METHOD

1 Remove the kernels from the cobs, reserving the cobs and kernels.

2 In a large stockpot, place the cobs, kernels, potatoes, celery, onion, carrots, and peppercorns and add water to cover. Bring to a boil over high heat, reduce to a simmer, and cook until the vegetables are soft, about 2 hours. Strain and cool. Transfer to a food-grade plastic or glass container. Will keep in fridge for 1 week and freezer for 4 months.

PRESSURE COOKER METHOD

Load the pressure cooker vessel with all the ingredients, lock the top, and cook on high pressure for 15 minutes.

FATS 7 AND OILS

One of the very best things about eating a bowl of great ramen is that lick-your-lips feeling that comes from the oils and fats that are used. After tending to your stock, you will cool it and pull off the fat cap to reserve it for when you assemble your bowl. Adding the fat back in may seem strange, but (like most Japanese cooking techniques) it's genius. First, it allows you to additionally season or combine oils to get a more robust flavor, and second, it's measured, so you know how much oil you have in each bowl.

There are some fats and oils that are added to the bowl during assembly that help create more viscosity and aroma, and there are others that are used on top of the ramen to add flavor and help shuttle the noodles down your gullet. The oils get the aroma going while you eat, help the noodles slide right into your mouth—and cover your face—as well as keep the ramen hot. Honestly, that's why ramen is a terrible date food. Listen to me, people: Your face and shirt will (and should) be covered in little bits of oil if you are crushing your bowl (see "How to Crush a Bowl of Ramen" on page 22).

Playing with oils in ramen is an area I think few people have really explored, and it's wide-open, as oil and infusion combinations are vast. On my last trip to Japan, I ate a bowl of ramen made with extra-virgin olive oil. It was fantastic. But as with all the chapters in this book, here I will show you the basics so you can begin to get wildly creative as you progress.

INFUSED FATS

// MAKES 1 CUP

In the ramen world, we use the fat that we skim off the top of the chintan (page 82) or paitan (page 88) to flavor the bowl when we're assembling (see page 154 for more on bowl assembly). One of the ways I like to add even more complex flavor is to infuse this fat with additional flavors from ingredients like garlic and ginger—but you can get creative with everything from bonito flakes to hot chiles.

CHICKEN FAT

You should have enough fat skimmed off the top of the cooled Tori Chintan (page 82) to yield 1 cup, but if you don't, you can fill out the cup with a neutral oil like grapeseed.

Garlic Chicken Fat

1 cup chicken fat

1 cup crushed garlic

Ginger Chicken Fat

1 cup chicken fat

1 cup coarsely chopped skin-on ginger

Sumac Chicken Fat

1 cup chicken fat

1 tablespoon ground sumac

1   In a small saucepan over low heat, combine the fat and the seasoning and cook for 1 hour.

2   Remove the pan from the heat and allow it to cool for about 5 minutes. Carefully strain the fat into a small airtight glass container. Discard the seasoning.

3   The fat will keep for 1 month in the refrigerator or 3 months in the freezer.

PORK FAT (HOT)

PORK FAT (COLD)

CHICKEN FAT (HOT)

CHICKEN FAT (COLD)

PORK FAT

After you strain and chill your tonkotsu (page 91), you will see the white fat cap. Remove it and try some of these infusions for your bowls. Our tonkotsu uses straight pork fat, no infusion, but it is topped with mayu, the burnt garlic oil that strikes a great bitter note up against all the porky fattiness.

1 cup niboshi (dried anchovies)

1 cup pork (page 105) or chicken fat (page 102)

Niboshi Oil
// MAKES ½ CUP

Bring the heat up slowly to 190°F and hold there for 10 minutes. Turn the heat off and allow to totally cool before straining niboshi out. Reserve the oil in the fridge.

½ cup garlic cloves

1 cup canola oil (or other high-heat neutral oil)

¼ cup sesame oil

Mayu (Burnt Garlic Oil)
// MAKES 2 CUPS

You read that right: burnt garlic. The first time I saw and tasted this was in Vancouver, on a cold, rainy day. A black slick on top of a very thick tonkotsu stock. It was so bitter, but I could not get enough. Mayu is meant to offset the fattiness of the broth. On its own, hard to eat. In tokotsu, perfection.

1 In a medium saucepan over medium-high heat, place the garlic cloves and sesame oil and cook, stirring occasionally to prevent the garlic from sticking, for about 20 minutes, until very dark brown. Remove the pan from the heat and allow it to cool to room temperature (the garlic should be black by the time it cools).

2 Place the mixture in a blender, in batches if needed, and blend on high until completely smooth.

3 Do not store this in the fridge; it will become a cement mass on the bottom and the oil will separate. The idea is to get this combination fully emulsified. The mayu will keep for up to 1 week in an airtight container.

FLAVORED OILS

Sometimes I am looking to add oil but not more animal fat, so I use a neutral oil like grapeseed and infuse it with other things to really bring that flavor and aroma directly to the bowl. You can also use canola if you prefer.

½ cup roughly chopped skin-on ginger

¼ cup roughly chopped scallions

1 cup sesame oil

1 cup grapeseed oil

GINGER SCALLION OIL
// MAKES 2 CUPS

1   In a 1- to 2-quart small saucepan affixed with a temperature gauge over medium heat, stir together the ginger, scallions, and the oils. Slowly raise the heat to 190 to 200°F. Keep the mixture at this temperature for 15 minutes, then remove the pan from the heat and allow the oil to cool.

2   Strain the oil into a small airtight glass container. The oil will keep for up to 1 month at room temperature.

2 cups grapeseed oil

½ cup Szechuan peppercorns

SZECHUAN PEPPERCORN OIL
// MAKES 2 CUPS

In a small saucepan affixed with a temperature gauge over medium heat, heat the oil to 190 to 200°F. Stir in the peppercorns and allow to steep for 1 hour. Strain the oil into a small glass airtight container. The oil will keep for up to 2 months.

2 cups grapeseed oil

1 cup roughly chopped garlic

GARLIC OIL
// MAKES 2 CUPS

In a small saucepan affixed with a temperature gauge over medium heat, heat the oil to 190 to 200°F. Stir in the garlic and allow to steep for 1 hour. Strain the oil into a small glass airtight container. The oil will keep for up to 2 months.

NIBOSHI OIL

SCALLION OIL

SZECHUAN PEPPERCORN OIL

GARLIC OIL

OTAKU RAYU 2.0

Many of the talented cooks and chefs who have worked with me over the years have been tasting and taking apart flavors to create something new since they started cooking. This is something I had to teach myself pretty much overnight when I decided to cook for a living . . . at forty-three. When I went to Sun Noodle to train with and learn from Naka, he gave me a taste of his rayu, and I have been trying to replicate it ever since. I could literally eat spoonfuls of it. I dream about it. This is the closest we have ever come to his.

3 tablespoons plus
    1½ teaspoons canola oil (or
    other high-heat neutral oil)

1 tablespoon plus
    2¼ teaspoons sesame oil

One 3-inch dried chile
    de árbol

¼ cup roughly chopped ginger

1 thinly sliced scallion
    (white part only)

½ cup gochujang
    (Korean chili paste)

¼ cup sesame seeds

¼ cup fried garlic

¼ cup fried onion

¼ cup Korean chili powder
    (see Note)

1 teaspoon soy sauce

1 teaspoon sugar

RAYU

// MAKES ABOUT 2½ CUPS

Although Japanese cuisine isn't generally known for its heat, rayu is an infused chile oil that's become increasingly popular as a dipping sauce and ramen topping in recent years. I love it because it's spicy, sweet, and texturally rich; and it's not so hot that it will leave you in physical pain. Rayu keeps well, which is convenient, because you'll find yourself putting it on everything from eggs to stir-fry.

1 In a medium saucepan over medium-high heat, combine the canola oil, sesame oil, chile de árbol, ginger, and scallion and cook until you start to smell the aroma, about 5 minutes.

2 Remove from the heat and fold in the gochujang, sesame seeds, fried garlic, fried onion, chili powder, soy sauce, and sugar. Let cool to room temperature.

3 Store in a small glass container with a tight-fitting lid. The rayu will keep for up to 1 week at room temperature or 1 month in the refrigerator.

Note

Korean chili powder is sometimes sold as "Korean red pepper flake powder" or "Korean red pepper fine powder."

SPICY MISO TARE

SHIO TARE

MISO TARE

SHOYU TARE

T
A
R
E

When you're making your grandma's chicken soup, you take the bones, water, and mirepoix (onion, celery, carrot) and cook them until you feel the broth is ready. Then you strain it, season it, serve it—and keep the leftovers in the refrigerator until they're finished. You will never treat ramen that way; all its elements should be kept separate until the moment you serve it. That's why there's so much diversity when it comes to ramen.

After you start making ramen, I dare say you will never make chicken soup the same way again.

In ramen, broth can define the style of the bowl, but tare defines the seasoning of the bowl. It is the main seasoning, alongside lesser elements that contribute to flavor.

Tare

Tare is the backbone of a bowl of ramen. Up until the moment you add tare, ramen broth is only bones and water—no salt, no mirepoix, no nothing—and tare is the main seasoning agent. It's what makes ramen a miso, shio, or shoyu ramen. Although most ramen chefs make their broth in a similar manner, it's the highly customized, highly prized tares that set ramen chefs apart from one another. These are basic recipes, but as you get more advanced, you can tinker with adding other elements, such as dried seafood and miso.

The most common tares are:

Shio—salt
Shoyu—soy
Miso—fermented beans or wheat

So when do you add your tare? There are infinite variations in the making of these tares, and they are most certainly what differentiate one ramen shop from another. You can season an entire batch of stock if you will be serving it that same day, but I don't recommend that you ever preseason a batch more than three hours before serving, because it can disrupt the emulsification, almost like a broken sauce. Plus, you may wake up the next day and decide you want to make another style of chicken soup with the remainder of your stock. Seasoning bowl by bowl is the way we do it in the shop and the way I suggest you do it, too, except when it comes to miso, which I will explain further.

Pro Tip: When you make the tare, I strongly recommend doubling or tripling the recipe to make a large batch. Tare is laborious to make, and the salt content allows it to keep for up to a year in a glass or plastic container in the refrigerator or frozen in a ziplock bag.

WHAT IS SALTY TO YOU IS PERFECT TO ME

You will hear me say this over and over: "What's salty to you is perfect to me." I will recommend how much tare to use per bowl, but as Ivan Orkin says, "I can't jump in your fucking mouth. I don't know what you taste." Point being, everyone's palate is different. You have to find the level of salt that works best for you and the ramen you are trying to make; adjustment is imperative to making the bowl balanced. Your salt could be saltier than mine, your soy stronger, etc., so just as we do in the shop, taste as you go, which is another reason that seasoning by the bowl rather than by the batch is a brilliant system.

This method works for all soup making for me now. I keep a batch of soup on the less salty side when I make it, and I season it more aggressively just before eating based on where my palate is that day. Some days you prefer a saltier soup than others.

SHOYU TARE

Shoyu tare is made of mainly soy sauce. It colors the broth, so it's not used quite as prevalently as shio. You can use an everyday soy like Kikkoman (I do), or if you have a more complex shoyu within your reach, try it. It's like cooking with good wine: the better the wine, the better the sauce. And all the other things that play in concert with the soy—the niboshi, the oil, the stock, the noodle—will enhance that flavor.

There are two ways to make this tare. I prefer the second because it's cleaner, but the first uses the Soy Marinade (page 137) from the Rolled Pork Belly (Chashu) and has a depth that the second does not. I recommend using HonDashi, a store-bought, freeze-dried dashi with a touch of MSG, because it distributes the flavors of kombu and bonito into the soy-based tare much better, unlike the shio. HonDashi can be found in any Asian market or online.

SOY MARINADE SHOYU TARE

// MAKES ABOUT 5 CUPS

2 cups Soy Marinade
(page 137)

2 cups soy sauce

½ cup drippings from
Rolled Pork Belly (Chashu)
(page 131; optional, if you
have it)

½ cup sea salt

¼ cup HonDashi

1. In a large stockpot over high heat, combine all the ingredients and bring the mixture to a boil. Allow the liquid to reduce to a volume of 4 cups—this is only about a 10 percent reduction, so it shouldn't take more than 10 minutes.

2. Using a blender or hand blender, emulsify the liquid. Allow the tare to cool, then cover tightly.

3. The tare will keep for 2 weeks in the refrigerator or up to 12 months in the freezer.

4. For instructions on serving tare with ramen, see page 111.

2 cups Sake Dashi (page 119)

2 tablespoons plus
1½ teaspoons rice vinegar

1 teaspoon kosher salt

1 tablespoon plus 1½ teaspoons
cane sugar

2 cups soy sauce

One 1-inch piece kombu

5 tablespoons sababushi
atsukezuri (dried mackerel
flake, thick cut)

5 tablespoons katsuobushi
atsukezuri (dried bonito
flake, thick cut)

2 teaspoons sake kasu (sake
lees)

Note:

**You can substitute 2 awase
dashi packets for the saba,
katsuo, and kombu.**

SHOYU TARE

// MAKES 4 CUPS

1   In a large stockpot affixed with a temperature gauge
over low heat, combine the sake dashi, rice vinegar, salt,
sugar, and soy sauce. Without allowing the temperature
to exceed 150°F, stir until the salt and sugar are
dissolved, then remove the pot from the heat.

2   Stir in the kombu, sababushi, and katsuobushi. Allow
the mixture to steep for up to 1 hour. Strain the
mixture, and stir the sake katsu into the liquid until it
dissolves.

3   The tare will keep for 2 weeks in the refrigerator or up
to 12 months in the freezer.

4   For instructions on serving tare with ramen, see
page 111.

Note:

These misos can be mixed together as well when you're making tare, so there are infinite options. Remember to document what you try so that if you strike gold you can replicate it.

1 cup white miso

½ cup kosher salt

½ cup water

6 tablespoons plus 1½ teaspoons tahini

¼ cup plus 1½ teaspoons sesame oil

2 tablespoons rice vinegar

2¼ teaspoons MSG

1 teaspoon ground white pepper

MISO TARE

Miso is the heartiest of all ramen. Think fortified miso soup with noodles in it (YUM): a stick-to-your-ribs kind of food that feels like a big warm blanket. Miso is also fermented, like the shoyu, so there is a lot of room for umami. Miso ramen is much thicker than the shio or shoyu simply because of the miso paste. I call for white miso in my tare, but you can try other types and see what you like. If you have good miso in your fridge already, use it.

Miso variations:

Shiro miso is on the sweeter side and is also called white miso. We typically use it for dressings.

Shinshu miso is fermented longer than shiro and has a richer flavor that makes it great for miso soup and ramen. This is our go-to.

Mugi miso is made from barley and is fermented a bit longer. It's much harder to find, but it can make for a really well-balanced and rich miso flavor. I would not use this miso your first time out, but definitely play with it if you find it.

AKA miso is red in color (due to longer fermentation time) and has a much saltier flavor.

MISO TARE

// MAKES 4 CUPS

1 In a large bowl, thoroughly mix together all the ingredients. Transfer to an airtight container.

2 The tare will keep for 2 weeks in the refrigerator or up to 12 months in the freezer.

3 For instructions on serving tare with ramen, see page 111.

1 cup white miso

½ cup sambal, or to taste

½ cup kosher salt

½ cup water

6 tablespoons plus
1½ teaspoons tahini

¼ cup plus 1½ teaspoons
sesame oil

¼ cup gochujang
(Korean chili paste)

2 tablespoons rice vinegar

2¼ teaspoons MSG

1 teaspoon ground white
pepper

SPICY MISO TARE
// MAKES 4 CUPS

This is one of those flavor combos you just never move away from if you love spice. It's simple, and you can adjust the heat to your liking by adding or taking away the sambal. In the shop, we make sure it has an intense kick. You might find other uses for this as well. Don't be afraid to toss it on chicken wings or make a salad dressing out of it by thinning it with oil and vinegar.

1 In a large bowl, thoroughly mix all the ingredients. Transfer to an airtight container.

2 The tare will keep for 2 weeks in the refrigerator or up to 12 months in the freezer.

3 For instructions on serving tare with ramen, see page 111.

1 cup chintan broth (page 82)

One 3-inch piece kombu

1 cup niboshi (dried anchovies)

2½ cups Sake Dashi (page 119)

2½ cups sea salt

2½ cups sake kasu (sake lees)

Note:

You can substitute 2 awase dashi packets for the sababushi, katsuobushi, and kombu.

SHIO TARE
// MAKES 4 CUPS

This Shio Tare is broth that is fortified with powerful umami-laden ingredients and is the most versatile of all tares. It's used in shio ramen and tonkotsu ramen, and it can be used as a base for more complex ramen like Curry Shio Ramen (page 175). Think of shio tare as Japanese bouillon.

1 In a stockpot affixed with a temperature gauge over medium heat, combine the chintan, kombu, and niboshi. Bring the mixture to 190°F and simmer for 1 hour. Remove the pot from the heat and allow it to cool for 10 minutes. Pass the liquid through a fine-mesh strainer with cheesecloth into a glass or a large plastic container.

2 Stir in the sake dashi and sea salt until the salt has dissolved. Allow the tare to cool, then cover tightly.

3 The tare will keep for 2 weeks in the refrigerator or up to 12 months in the freezer.

4 For instructions on serving tare with ramen, see page 111.

SAKE DASHI // MAKES ABOUT 4 CUPS

Sake dashi is a valuable building block for all tares, helping to fortify your tare and give it more depth.

4 cups sake

¼ cup sababushi atsukezuri (dried mackerel flake, thick cut)

¼ cup katsuobushi atsukezuri (dried bonito flake, thick cut)

15 grams kombu

2 tablespoons dried shiitake mushrooms

1 In a large saucepan affixed with a temperature gauge over medium-high heat, stir together all the ingredients and bring to a light boil. Reduce the heat and let steep for 1 hour at 190°F.

2 Alternatively, you can stir together the ingredients, let the mixture sit overnight, then bring to a boil and immediately remove from the heat.

3 Taste the saba and katsuo; if they no longer have a fishy flavor, then you know the dashi is ready.

TOPPINGS

The final layer of a bowl of ramen is the topping. Some toppings are meant to punctuate the bowl, while others are meant to complement it. I've given you a range of options to choose from—some are standard, like the chashu (rolled pork belly), and others are unique to Otaku Ramen shop, like the Pork Confit.

Do not be afraid to go off course here, either. This is where ramen can become regional and personal. I had a cook from Florida who wanted to make alligator ramen. It worked. I have seen crawfish ramen. Tofu three ways. You get the picture. Get creative here as you stroll the aisles of your Asian market or simply use what you have in the fridge.

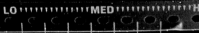

WARNING:
INDUCTION RANGE IN USE
SURFACE MAY BE HOT

VOLLRATH®

Intrigue

HEAT
TEMP

LO | MED | HI

| 140 | 175 | 285 | 320 | 355 | 390 | 430 | °F |
| 60 | 80 | 140 | 160 | 180 | 200 | 220 | °C |

HEATING

ON
OFF

VOLLRATH®

INDUCTION
1440W @ 120V

2 skinless, boneless chicken
  breasts

2 tablespoons shio koji

1 tablespoon canola oil (or
  other high-heat neutral oil)

KOJI CHICKEN BREAST

// SERVES 4

This recipe is going to change your life as a cook. I am not being dramatic. Game changer. I could write a book (I might) on the use of shio koji. It's dead simple and the payoff is giant. "Koji'd" rice is the base you begin with when you make sake or miso. Shio koji is made from fermented rice, water, and salt—it ends up looking a bit like rice pudding. As in this recipe, the salt and starch in shio koji can act as a tenderizer for your protein of choice. If you prefer, you can swap the chicken for pork tenderloin or practically any cut of beef.

1 In a ziplock bag (or glass or plastic container), place the chicken breasts and coat with the shio koji. Squeeze out all the air and make sure the koji surrounds the meat on all sides. Refrigerate for at least 2 hours and up to 24 hours.

2 Preheat the oven to 325°F.

3 Remove the chicken from the bag, lightly rinse off the koji, and pat dry.

4 In an oven-safe skillet over medium-high heat, heat the oil. Sear the chicken, about 5 minutes per side.

5 Place the skillet in the oven and cook until the internal temperature of the chicken reaches 175°F, about 10 minutes. Allow the meat to rest for 10 to 15 minutes before slicing or shredding.

6 Assemble the bowl according to the recipe instructions.

2 cups sake

2 cups water

2 cups chintan broth
(page 82)

2 teaspoons kosher or sea salt

One 2-inch piece skin-on
ginger, thinly sliced

1 tablespoon coarsely chopped
garlic

2 skinless boneless chicken
breasts

POACHED CHICKEN BREAST

// SERVES 4

I serve this with a shio or tori paitan ramen, and it's meant to complement, not overpower, the bowl.

1 In a large pot affixed with a temperature gauge over high heat, combine the sake, water, chintan, salt, ginger, and garlic. Bring the poaching liquid to a simmer, then drop in the chicken and simmer until cooked through (190°F on your temperature gauge), about 20 minutes.

2 Remove from the heat and allow the chicken to cool in the poaching liquid.

3 Once cooled, slice the chicken to the desired thickness. We prefer a ¼-inch thickness on the bias to create longer slices. Bring the chicken to room temperature before adding it to the ramen.

4 Assemble the bowl according to the recipe instructions.

1 cup salt

½ cup sugar

4 skinless, boneless chicken thighs

2 cups chicken fat (page 102); or any other animal fat

½ cup garlic cloves

1 medium onion, halved

1 lemon, quartered

CHICKEN CONFIT

// SERVES 4

Made with thighs, this recipe gives you a rich, silky piece of chicken that can be sliced or shredded for your bowl of choice. We use this on both shio and paitan in the shop.

1   In a large ziplock bag, mix together the salt and sugar. Place the chicken in the bag and coat with the mixture. Refrigerate for at least 12 hours and up to 3 days.

2   Rinse the salt and sugar from the chicken. In a large skillet affixed with a temperature gauge over medium-high heat, place the chicken, fat, garlic, onion, and lemon. Cook at 225°F for 3 hours, or until the internal temperature of the chicken reaches 180°F. Remove the skillet from the heat and allow to cool. Pull out the chicken, reserving the fat for ramen. Slice or shred the meat when it has completely cooled.

3   Assemble the bowl according to the recipe instructions.

2 pounds skin-on boneless chicken thighs

1 teaspoon dried shiitake mushroom powder

2 tablespoons minced peeled ginger

2 tablespoons minced garlic

1 cup minced scallions (green and white parts)

2 teaspoons cornstarch

2 teaspoons salt

¾ cup panko bread crumbs

MEATBALL MIX
// SERVES 4

We could never get meatballs to look pretty on the ramen, so we just serve this as crumbled meatballs. This mix is so delicious and so versatile, it somehow ended up in my Thanksgiving dressing last year.

1   In a food processor fitted with a sharp blade, place the chicken and mushroom powder and pulse until the chicken is ground. Remove the blade attachment and affix the mixer attachment.

2   Add the remaining ingredients and pulse until thoroughly mixed. Refrigerate for at least 1 hour.

3   If you're making meatballs: Preheat the oven to 350°F.

4   After the meat has rested, form the mixture into 1-inch meatballs. Bake for about 20 minutes, until the meatballs are lightly browned with a steamed texture and cooked through.

5   If you're not making meatballs: In a skillet over high heat, cook the ground meat until browned and slightly crispy on the outside, about 10 minutes total.

6   Assemble the bowl according to the recipe instructions.

One 5- to 8-pound pork belly

One 4-inch piece skin-on
ginger, cut into rough slices

3 star anise

4 tablespoons canola oil (or
other high-heat neutral oil)

1¼ cups soy sauce

1¼ cups mirin

1¼ cups sake

½ cup water

2 tablespoons sugar

CHASHU (ROLLED PORK BELLY)

// MAKES 25 TO 30 ½-INCH-THICK SLICES, DEPENDING ON SIZE OF BELLY

This is the most traditional version of a chashu you will find. Sliced and rolled pork belly is one of the most iconic visuals of a great ramen bowl.

1 Preheat the oven to 350°F.

2 Cut the pork in half to create two square pieces. Roll tightly and secure with butcher twine.

3 In a cheesecloth sachet, place the ginger and star anise. Tie the sachet and set aside.

4 In a sauté pan over high heat, heat the oil and sear the outside of the pork belly roll. Set the pork aside in a braising pan.

5 In a medium saucepan over high heat, bring the soy sauce, mirin, sake, water, and sugar to a boil. Pour the mixture over the seared pork and add the sachet of ginger and star anise.

6 Place the pork in the oven and braise for 45 minutes. Remove the ginger and star anise sachet and cover the pan with aluminum foil. Reduce the heat to 250°F and braise for 3 hours and 15 minutes more, or until tender. Remove the pork from the oven and allow it to cool. Cool completely in the refrigerator before slicing.

7 Assemble the bowl according to the recipe instructions.

Note

Reserve the braising liquid for making Soy Marinade Shoyu Tare (page 114). This can be made well in advance and stored in the fridge until it's time to serve.

MARINADE:

1 cup Soy Marinade (page 137)

1 cup water

1 cup skin-on, roughly chopped ginger

1 cup chopped garlic

5 star anise

2 cinnamon sticks

5 cloves

5 pounds pork belly

SOY PORK BELLY

**// MAKES ONE 5-POUND PIECE
(ENOUGH FOR ABOUT 10 RAMEN BOWLS)**

This is a great alternative to the traditional rolled pork belly known as chashu (page 131). It's a little easier to make at home and offers the same great flavor. We use this in the ramen shop for the pork buns and to top several of our ramen bowls, particularly those with a paitan broth (page 88), whose mellow flavor pairs well with the sweet, succulent roasted pork.

1 Combine all the marinade ingredients in a large ziplock bag. Add the pork to the bag. Squeeze the air out and massage the liquid across the surface of the pork. Refrigerate the bag for at least 12 hours and up to 24 hours.

2 Preheat the oven to 350°F.

3 Remove the pork from the marinade and place it in a tight-fitting glass or metal baking dish. Cover and cook for 3 hours and 30 minutes to 4 hours. You will know it's done when the meat easily pulls away with a fork.

4 Cover the pork and chill it in the refrigerator until you're ready to serve.

5 To serve: Plan on serving two slices of pork per bowl of ramen. Cut the chilled pork into ¼-inch-thick slices. About 5 minutes before assembling the bowl of ramen, heat a small sauté pan over medium-high and sear each slice, flipping once, for about 30 seconds on each side. Set the seared pork aside.

6 Assemble the bowl according to the recipe instructions.

Note

As the pork is easier to slice when cold, it's ideal to make this in advance. The pork will keep, covered, for up to 5 days in the refrigerator or 2 months in the freezer.

3 pounds pork butt, cut into
  2-inch cubes

1½ cups canola oil (or other
  high-heat neutral oil)

5 tablespoons salt

5 tablespoons sugar

PORK CONFIT

// SERVES 6

This is what we use on our Tennessee Tonkotsu in the shop, and I have become really fond of this style of protein on a ramen. After cooking and cooling the confit, we scoop it onto the griddle and let it get crispy on the outside.

1   Preheat the oven to 200°F.

2   Arrange the meat in a large baking pan.

3   In a large saucepan over medium-high heat, heat 1 cup of the oil. Stir in the salt and sugar until they dissolve, then turn off the heat. Add the remaining ½ cup of oil and stir. Pour the oil over the meat and cover with aluminum foil.

4   Cook in the oven for 6 hours, or until the pork falls apart easily when pierced with a fork.

5   Allow the meat to cool, then pour off the oil, reserving it for another use.

6   Shred the pork and form the meat into ¼-inch balls that you will sear in a sauté pan before serving.

7   Assemble the bowl according to the recipe instructions.

8   The pork will keep for 1 week in the refrigerator or 6 months in the freezer.

1 tablespoon canola oil (or other high-heat neutral oil)

2 pounds ground pork

1 tablespoon freshly ground Szechuan peppercorns

Salt, to taste

SZECHUAN GROUND PORK

// SERVES 4

Also a very common topping in the ramen game, you will see ground pork on tantanmen-style ramen most times, but our variation with Szechuan peppercorns gives it extra kick and spice. This peppercorn plays with the tongue a little, slightly anesthetizing it to allow spicy flavors in without burning your palate out. It's the key to spicy Szechuan food and works really well in ramen.

1 In a large skillet over medium-high heat, heat the oil. Add the ground pork and spread it out as thin as the skillet will allow. Add the peppercorn and let the pork cook until it begins to crisp a little. Stir the pork until it is cooked through, 5 to 10 minutes. Season with salt.

2 Assemble the bowl according to the recipe instructions.

2 cups cooking sake

1 cup mirin

3 cups soy sauce

3 cups peeled and minced
fresh ginger

1 cup coarsely chopped garlic

⅔ cup sugar

SOY MARINADE (AKA SSM)

// MAKES 6 CUPS

This is a salty-sweet marinade that I use for both the Soy Eggs (page 147) and the Soy Pork Belly (page 132), including in the base of ponzu and in the tare on page 114. It comes together in minutes, making what my cooks call SSM (soy, sake, mirin). This is one of my favorite all-purpose sauces to have on hand.

1 In a medium saucepan over high heat, place the sake and mirin. Boil for 3 to 4 minutes to burn off their alcohol. Add the soy sauce, ginger, garlic, and sugar and simmer, stirring occasionally, for 10 minutes.

2 Remove the pan from the heat and allow it to cool to room temperature.

3 Strain out the ginger and garlic and reserve the remaining sauce, covered in the refrigerator, for up to 1 month.

2 pounds Napa cabbage, shredded

4 scallions (green and white parts divided)

¼ cup salt

¼ cup plus 2 tablespoons chopped garlic

3 tablespoons fresh peeled and chopped ginger

¼ cup Korean chili powder

¼ cup red AKA miso

¼ cup water

2 tablespoons sugar

2 tablespoons soy sauce

½ pound daikon, pureed

VEGAN KIMCHI

// MAKES 4 CUPS

This kimchi recipe is as simple as they come, and super versatile. This is a constant in my fridge and can make a midnight meal of rice a hundred times better. This is what we use in our spicy miso at the shop.

1   Rinse the cabbage and scallion greens, then place them in a large container and add the salt.

2   In a food processor, puree the scallion whites, garlic, ginger, chili powder, miso, water, sugar, and soy sauce until smooth.

3   In a large glass container, mix together the cabbage, scallion greens, pureed daikon, and scallion paste. Cover and leave the mixture at room temperature for at least 2 days.

4   The kimchi will keep for up to 3 months in the refrigerator.

A TALE OF TWO SCALLION (CUTTERS)

I have a tendency to get carried away on Instagram some nights, as I find stunning bowl after stunning bowl of ramen to gawk at. In my own shop, I often question the composition of my bowls. Could they look better? Do they look messy? And good god why do the scallions look so messy?! I want pretty scallions for my ramen.

This obsession led me on an expedition of epic proportions to Kappabashi, the restaurant-supply area of Tokyo, to buy a scallion cutter. Okay, maybe two scallion cutters. (See, they do everything better in Japan, and I kept looking at all the beautiful scallions on their bowls, and damn it, I wanted my scallions to look like that.)

The first thing you need to know is that the Japanese version of a scallion is (of course) much better than ours. It's called *negi*, and it's as if a leek and a scallion had a baby. More white than green, and it has a much milder flavor. These Japanese machines are made for *negi*, not scallions. But I persisted because I had to have this cutter.

We had two hours of translated back-and-forth about the types of cutters, the capabilities of the cutters, and the fact that if we buy them, they won't ship them for us because of the blade, and we can't order another blade if this one breaks. Rules, rules, rules. No matter—we bought the scallion cutter and it makes my heart whir with delight. Two kinds: rounds and threads.

However, you and your very sharp knife can achieve beautiful scallions for your own ramen at home. Here is how.

2 cups water (or mushroom liquid from reconstituting shiitakes or wood ears below)

1 cup sugar

1 cup sherry vinegar

1 cup usukuchi (light soy sauce)

Two 3-inch pieces fresh ginger, peeled

4 cups reconstituted dried shiitakes or wood ears

PICKLED SHIITAKES OR WOOD EARS

// MAKES 4 CUPS

This is an adaptation from the Momofuku cookbook, and hands down it's one of my favorite things in the universe. I'd like to personally thank the Momofuku team for not only teaching me a brilliant way to reuse the shiitakes from our vegetable broth (hint, hint), but also for making my daughter a lifelong lover of the fungi with these. Not only do we use these in the shop on various ramen, but we fight over them at staff meals. In my house we have been known to eat these with a bowl of rice and a poached egg with a pinch of shichimi togarashi (a common red chili spice mix used as a topping). And of course they make an excellent topping for any ramen.

1   In a large saucepan over medium-low heat, place the water, sugar, vinegar, usukuchi, and ginger and simmer gently for 30 minutes, until the flavors have married. Discard the ginger.

2   In a glass or plastic container, place the shiitakes or wood ears and pour the hot liquid over. Allow to cool slightly before placing in the fridge. The mushrooms will keep, covered, for up to 3 months in the refrigerator.

VEGETABLES

They can play a starring role or a supporting role, but vegetables are what complete a bowl of ramen, no matter how minimal. I think that is one of my favorite things about Japanese ramen. Toppings and especially vegetables are used not only for taste (find cabbage on the umami chart, why don't you . . . See?!) but for the composition of a bowl as well.

Here are some simple vegetable topping ideas to get the wheels turning:

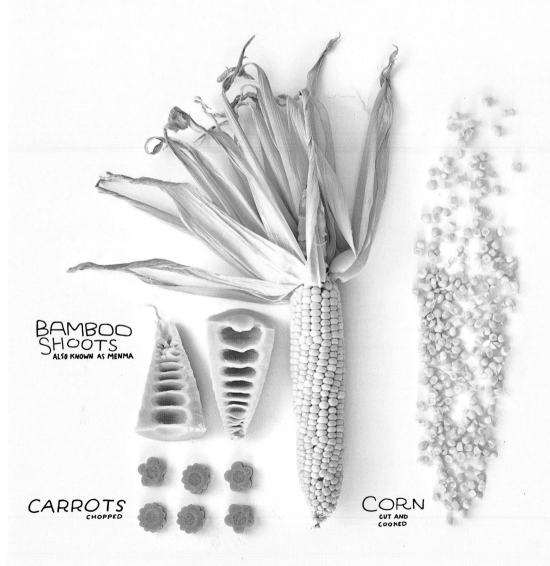

BAMBOO
SHOOTS
ALSO KNOWN AS MENMA

CARROTS
CHOPPED

CORN
CUT AND
COOKED

SWEET
POTATO
ROASTED

ENOKI
MUSHROOM
RAW

WOOD EAR
MUSHROOM
OR SOMETIMES SIMPLY
CALLED BLACK FUNGUS

CABBAGE
SHREDDED AND SALTED
(ADDS A NICE BITE)

SPROUTS
MUNG BEAN SPROUTS

GREENS
BLANCHED SPINACH,
TURNIP GREENS,
FRESH MIZUNA

GARLIC RAW
CHIPS
ROASTED

1 cup Soy Marinade
  (page 137)

2 cups cold water

12 ramen eggs (page 148)

SOY EGGS

// MAKES 12 EGGS

Known as *ajitsuke tamago* in Japanese, this variation of the Ramen Egg is marinated in a delicious salty-sweet soy sauce (it's the same marinade I use on the Soy Pork Belly on page 132). You can let them soak for a little longer than 12 hours, but don't go too long, or the salt will begin to denature the egg and give it an unappealing hard texture.

1   In a bowl or container large enough to submerge all the eggs, stir together the Soy Marinade and water. Add the peeled ramen eggs (page 148) and allow the eggs to marinate for 12 hours, turning the eggs occasionally to ensure even steeping.

2   To serve on ramen, cut the egg in half and float it yolk-side up in the bowl (for more on ramen bowl assembly, see page 154).

12 large eggs

1 cup white vinegar

½ cup kosher salt

RAMEN EGGS

// MAKES 12 EGGS

Eggs are a common topping for all different kinds of ramen—some ramen shops add them automatically, while others offer them as an add-on, which I almost always opt for. Ramen eggs should have a white that's completely set, with a creamy yolk that's almost the texture of marmalade. Even if you're not making ramen, these are a great and easy snack to have on hand at home. You'll never go back to hard-boiling after mastering this technique.

1 Pull the eggs out of the refrigerator and let them sit out for at least 1 hour to come to room temperature.

2 Bring a large pot with enough water to cover all the eggs (roughly 12 cups) to a boil over high heat. While the water comes to a boil, set up an ice bath in a large bowl with about 3 cups of ice cubes and 10 cups of cold water, ideally in your sink. Add the vinegar to the boiling water.

3 Once the water reaches a rolling boil, carefully lower in all the eggs and set a timer for 8 minutes.

4 When the timer buzzes, remove the eggs and immediately sink them in the ice bath.

5 At this point, you can keep the unpeeled eggs in the refrigerator for up to 5 days. For ramen purposes, you'll want to peel the eggs in advance of serving so you can assemble everything quickly (for more on ramen assembly instructions, see page 154). Peeled eggs will keep, floating in a container of cool water, in the refrigerator for up to 2 days.

8
MINUTES

RAMEN
EGGS

10
MINUTES

10
RAMEN
STYLES
AND RECIPES

This is where the rubber meets the road. You have learned the fundamentals of how to build a great bowl, and you are ready to show your friends that you can indeed make a serious bowl of ramen. There are new styles of ramen being created every day. They are all based on one of the four base flavors in a chintan (clear broth), paitan (cloudy broth), or sometimes even a combination. First let's explore the most basic recipes. Then I'll give you some classic and beloved regional styles from Japan, and finally, my own styles and recipes from the Otaku Ramen shop.

Regional ramen is a term used in Japan and the U.S. as a catchall phrase akin to the term *farm-to-table*. The concept is that styles of ramen have evolved or been created based on where the ramen is from. I like to think that a bowl of ramen is unique to the place where it is made, and in a sense it always is, simply because of the ingredients used (bones, water, etc.). When I first began making ramen, I chose to make tonkotsu, and by using Tennessee pork bones and topping it with shredded pork, I paid a little homage to Tennessee-style pulled pork barbecue. A great example of Japanese regional ramen is from a shop on Rishiri Island, north of Hokkaido. The shop uses a large amount of Rishiri kelp, some of the most expensive kelp in the world, and which is specific to that region of Japan. It's a shoyu style, but the umami from the kelp makes this particular bowl very unique and truly regional.

On the other hand, a bowl does not need to be tied to its *terroir* to be great. The region a ramen comes from tells part of the story but not all of it. The rest of the story belongs to the cook. Begin by looking for local bones, and as you learn more about the basics of ramen, you, too, will be able to incorporate ingredients and techniques that make your ramen regional. If you live in Kansas City, maybe you need to make a "Burnt Ends Ramen" (please call me if you do; I'd like to eat that). Another great ramen shop in the U.S., Ramen Tatsu-Ya in Austin, makes a brisket mazemen that blows minds—a brilliant marriage of local Texan flavors and Japanese technique.

These recipes are meant to demonstrate the most basic versions of each ramen.

RAMEN
BOWL
ASSEMBLY

When it comes to serving, the best way to approach ramen is to think of yourself as a one-person assembly line. You want everything—your serving bowls, broth, fat, noodles, and toppings—to be within reach so you can assemble your bowl as quickly as possible. The moment the noodles hit the boiling water, the clock is ticking. The key here is proper organization.

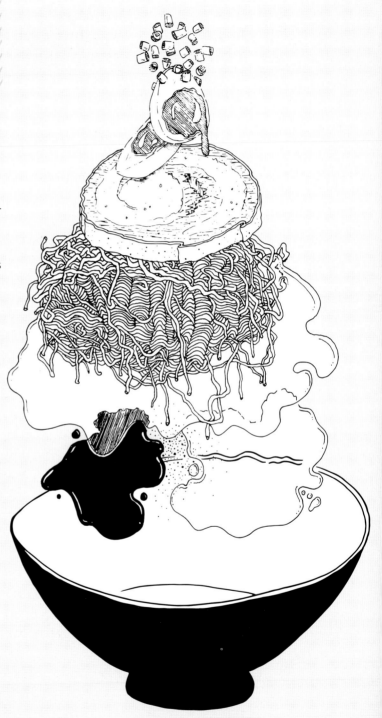

1 Get your biggest pot going three-quarters of the way full of water to a boil, ideally with a strainer that fits into it (or a double boiler with holes in it), in order to cook the noodles—more on that in a second. Make sure your serving bowls and all toppings, tare, and fats are laid out for easy access.

2 Add the tare and fat and dried powders to each serving bowl.

3 While the noodles boil, heat the stock in a separate large pot over medium heat to 190°F (do not boil it).

4 If one of your toppings is the Soy Pork Belly (page 132) or Rolled Pork Belly (page 131), now is the time to pull out a sauté pan and sear your slices for 30 seconds on each side. Set aside while the noodles cook.

5 Now is also a good time to peel and cut the Ramen Eggs (page 148) in half, if using.

6 Cook the noodles according to the package instructions, minus a few seconds of cooking time, as the noodles will continue to cook in the hot broth. In the restaurant, we use noodle cages to keep individual noodle portions separate, but at home, it's easier to use a strainer, which allows you to pull the noodles out of the boiling water quickly and cleanly—very important in ramen assembly, where every second counts.

7 When the noodles have about 30 seconds of cooking time left, ladle the stock into each bowl. When the noodles are done, pull the strainer containing them out of the hot water, and using chopsticks, divide the noodles among the serving bowls, into four even portions, working as quickly as you can.

8 Once the noodles are in the soup, use chopsticks to lightly stir them around, so that stock and fat evenly coat each noodle. Then grab as many noodles as possible with your chopsticks, pull them upward out of the stock, and lay them flat across the top, creating a sort of raft for the proteins and vegetables.

9 Add your toppings and serve immediately!

CHEF INTERVIEW:
Yuji Haraguchi (Okonomi, Yuji Ramen)

\\\

Where did you grow up in Japan and what was the main style of ramen there?

I grew up in Utsunomiya, Tochigi. The city is known for gyoza, not ramen. There are a lot of gyoza restaurants [there] where you get only two or three different types (boiled, fried, and pan seared) of gyoza, rice, and beer . . .

Tell me what it was like working for the Tsukiji Fish Market of Tokyo out of NY? Is this where you learned so much about fish?

I worked at a Japanese seafood company that imported fish from Tsukiji. I learned that the quality of Japanese seafood comes a lot from the philosophy of how they handle and take care of ingredients in Japan. If we import just that philosophy instead of actual products, we can develop amazing Japanese food cultures in the U.S. with local ingredients here.

When did you make your first serious bowl of ramen?

I think 2011 . . . Until then I didn't eat ramen at all.

When I started thinking about my first ramen pop-up, I visited your stall at Smorgasburg in Brooklyn. How did that all begin for you?

I thought that it was important to test [my] creations and build customers before having my own restaurant. I tried to offer at least one new dish every weekend. Having YUJI Ramen ramen stand at Smorgasburg every weekend was the best way to do it. Also, it allowed me to work at a restaurant during the week, as I had never worked in the restaurant before.

Mazemen was the first style you offered. How did you find that style, and what inspired you?

When I started making ramen in 2011, I had no idea how to make good broth and struggled. I bought many ramen cookbooks and nothing made sense to me . . . but when I discovered mazemen, I got so excited because I was able to link it with the Japanese-style pasta, which I was good at making and loved eating. My very first part-time job in college was actually a server at a Japanese Italian restaurant. So I tested a lot of flavors from my memories of eating there with ramen noodles instead of pasta. At that time, no one was doing mazemen at all in the U.S. I didn't care how good my mazemen would be for customers that time. I just wanted to be the first one doing it. I also thought that mazemen will make ramen more accessible for a lot of people here. I noticed that slurping hot noodle in hot broth was not easy for American customers.

What do you think the biggest differences are between ramen in the U.S. and ramen in Japan?

It's definitely the perception on what the ramen should be. Japanese people are very particular about what it should be and don't always go outside of what's familiar to them. But American customers will accept any style of ramen as long as it's good. That's why I enjoy making ramen here in the U.S. and wanted to create new ramen cultures here.

What's the most extreme interpretation of ramen that you have eaten? Can it go too far and break too many rules?

I believe in new creations for traditional cuisines. But at the same time, it's important to be within the limitations and rules that define the cuisine. If I see extreme styles of ramen that [don't] make sense to me, I just don't eat it . . .

What's the ramen secret you wish everyone could know?
It's "mottainai."

Where in the world (outside of Japan) do you see the most exciting ramen being created?
At Otaku Ramen in Nashville!

MAZEMEN

Mazemen is a newer style of ramen that literally means "mix it up" in Japanese. It is described as a brothless ramen style that is served either warm or cold and contains more of a sauce than a broth. Ivan Ramen's Triple Garlic Mazemen and Yuji Haraguchi's Bacon and Egg Mazemen are some of the most incredible-tasting ramen I have ever had. The Sicilian in me wants to make mazemen a lot, and I find myself experimenting with a crossroads of flavors in this style more than others.

Note

This recipe assumes that you have broth, tare, and fats already made. From there, plan to make all the toppings before assembling bowls. (For more on ramen assembly instructions, see page 154.)

EQUIPMENT NEEDED

Large pot for blanching greens

Large bowl for ice bath

Large stockpot with strainer or double boiler with holes

Large pot for broth

FOR TOPPINGS:

1 Koji Chicken Breast, sliced or shredded (page 123)

2 cups greens, such as whole-leaf spinach, bok choy, mustard greens, or turnip greens

2 Ramen Eggs (page 148)

4 tablespoons thinly sliced scallions (green parts only)

FOR RAMEN:

8 tablespoons Shio Tare (page 119; best made at least 1 day in advance)

4 tablespoons Ginger Chicken Fat (page 102)

4 pinches fish powder (ground katsuobushi)

4 pinches ground white pepper

SHIO RAMEN

// MAKES 4 BOWLS

Shio (salt) ramen is the Japanese version of Grandma's chicken soup. It's deceptively simple, but when it's done right, it's the most soothing soup there is. Most shops use pork in the broth and the toppings, but I prefer to keep this recipe all chicken. You can vary the recipe by subbing pork fat, pork chashu, etc.

This ramen is what we call a double soup, as it has chintan broth and dashi mixed together, and it's a prime example of simple yet powerful umami.

1   Bring the chicken to room temperature.

2   Blanch the greens: In a large pot, bring 4 quarts of water to a boil. Prepare an ice bath in a large bowl.

3   The idea is to poach the whole leaf, stem included, for presentation and texture. When the water is boiling, add the greens and cook for about 30 seconds. Immediately plunge the greens into the ice water, pat them dry, and lay the leaves vertically next to one another on a cutting board. Cut the leaves into 2-inch strips and set aside.

ASSEMBLY:

4   Fill your biggest pot three-quarters full with water over high heat to bring the water to a boil, ideally with a strainer (or double boiler with holes) that fits into it.

5   Meanwhile, make sure your serving bowls and all toppings, tare, and fats are laid out for easy access.

6   Place 2 tablespoons of the tare, 1 tablespoon of the chicken fat, 1 pinch of the fish powder, and 1 pinch of the pepper into each individual serving bowl.

recipe and ingredients continue >

4 cups chintan broth
(page 82)

2 cups dashi broth, combined
with chintan broth
(page 97; must be made
2 days in advance)

18 ounces fresh ramen
noodles, or 12 ounces dried

7 In a separate large pot affixed with a temperature gauge over medium heat, combine the chintan and the dashi and heat the broth to 190°F (do not boil).

8 Slice the ramen eggs in half and set aside.

9 Cook the noodles according to the package instructions, minus a few seconds of cooking time, as the noodles will continue to cook in the hot broth.

10 When the noodles have about 30 seconds of cooking time left, ladle 1½ cups of broth into each bowl. When the noodles are done, pull the strainer containing them out of the hot water, and using chopsticks, divide the noodles as evenly as possible among the serving bowls, working as quickly as you can.

11 Once the noodles are in, use chopsticks to lightly stir them around, so that the broth and fat evenly coat each noodle. Then grab as many noodles as possible, pull them upward out of the broth, and lay them flat across the top, creating a sort of raft on which to lay the toppings.

12 To each bowl, add 1 cup of the shredded chicken, ¼ cup of the blanched greens, 1 tablespoon of the scallions, and half an egg. Serve immediately.

Note

This recipe assumes that you have broth, tare, and fats already made. From there, plan to make all the toppings before assembling bowls. (For more on ramen assembly instructions, see page 154.)

EQUIPMENT NEEDED

Large pot for blanching greens

Large bowl for ice bath

Large stockpot with strainer or double boiler with holes

Large pot for broth

FOR TOPPINGS:

4 slices Rolled Pork Belly (Chashu) (page 131)

2 cups greens, such as whole-leaf spinach, bok choy, mustard greens, or turnip greens

2 Soy Eggs (page 147)

4 tablespoons thinly sliced scallions (green parts only)

4 (1 x 4-inch) sheets roasted nori

FOR RAMEN:

8 tablespoons Shoyu Tare (page 115; best made at least 1 day in advance)

4 tablespoons chicken fat (page 102)

4 tablespoons Niboshi Oil (page 105)

4 pinches ground white pepper

SHOYU RAMEN

// SERVES 4

Shoyu (soy) ramen is my go-to bowl. It's bright and flavorful, and if it's well balanced, the umami is outstanding. In other words, it's a very satisfying ramen.

Like the shio, the shoyu is also a double soup. The dashi, although it doesn't seem like a key ingredient, adds amino acids, creating pure umami when it's combined with the soy.

1 Bring the chashu to room temperature.

2 Blanch the greens: In a large pot, bring 4 quarts of water to a boil. Prepare an ice bath in a large bowl.

3 The idea is to poach the whole leaf, stem included, for presentation and texture. When the water is boiling, add the greens and cook for about 30 seconds. Immediately plunge the greens into the ice water, pat them dry, and lay the leaves vertically next to one another on a cutting board. Cut the leaves into 2-inch strips and set aside.

ASSEMBLY:

4 Fill your biggest pot three-quarters full with water over high heat to bring the water to a boil, ideally with a strainer (or double boiler with holes) that fits into it. Meanwhile, make sure your serving bowls and all toppings, tare, and fats are laid out for easy access. Mark each serving bowl with 2 tablespoons of the tare, 1 tablespoon of the fat, 1 tablespoon of the niboshi oil, 1 pinch of the pepper, and 1 pinch of the fish powder.

5 In a separate large pot affixed with a temperature gauge over medium heat, combine the chintan and the dashi and heat the broth to 190°F (do not boil).

recipe and ingredients continue >

4 pinches of ground
katsuobushi (page 43)

4 cups chintan broth
(page 82)

2 cups dashi broth
(page 97; must be made
2 days in advance)

18 ounces fresh ramen
noodles or 12 ounces dried

6 Slice the soy eggs in half and set aside.

7 Cook the noodles according to the package
instructions, minus a few seconds of cooking time,
as the noodles will continue to cook in the hot broth.

8 When the noodles have about 30 seconds of cooking
time left, ladle 1½ cups of broth into each bowl. When
the noodles are done, pull the strainer containing them
out of the hot water, and using chopsticks, divide the
noodles as evenly as possible among the serving bowls,
working as quickly as you can.

9 Once the noodles are in, use chopsticks to lightly stir
them around, so that the broth and fat evenly coat
each noodle. Then grab as many noodles as possible,
pull them upward out of the broth, and lay them flat
across the top, creating a sort of raft on which to lay
the toppings.

10 To each bowl, add 1 slice of the chashu, ¼ cup of the
blanched greens, 1 tablespoon of the scallions, half an
egg, and 1 sheet of the nori. Serve immediately.

Note

This recipe assumes that you have broth, tare, and fats already made. From there, plan to make all the toppings before assembling your bowls. (For more on ramen assembly instructions, see page 154.)

EQUIPMENT NEEDED

Small skillet

Large stockpot with strainer or double boiler with holes

Large pot for broth

FOR TOPPINGS:

1 tablespoon canola oil (or other high-heat neutral oil) for confit

2 tablespoons Mayu (Burnt Garlic Oil) (page 105)

1 cup Pork Confit (page 135)

¾ cup Pickled Wood Ear mushrooms (page 142)

4 tablespoons thinly sliced scallions (green parts only)

2 Ramen Eggs (page 148)

FOR RAMEN:

8 tablespoons Shio Tare (page 119; best made at least 1 day in advance)

4 tablespoons pork fat (page 105)

4 pinches ground white pepper

TENNESSEE TONKOTSU RAMEN

// MAKES 4 BOWLS

This is the mother lode of ramen. Directly translated, *tonkotsu* means "pork bone," and that's what this is: pork bone ramen. This version is called the Tennessee Tonkotsu, where I conceived this bowl and serve it.

This is what you want when you need ramen; it's hearty and it sticks to your ribs.

1 In a small skillet over high heat, heat ½ tablespoon of canola oil. Add 4 separate ¼-cup scoops of the confit to the skillet and flatten slightly to create a crisp surface. Cook for 3 to 4 minutes per side, or until golden brown, and set aside.

2 Submerge the wood ear mushrooms in hot water for 10 minutes, or until soft. Drain, cut the mushrooms into slivers, and set aside.

ASSEMBLY:

3 Fill your biggest pot three-quarters full with water over high heat to bring the water to a boil, ideally with a strainer (or double boiler with holes) that fits into it. Meanwhile, make sure your serving bowls and all toppings, tare, and fats are laid out for easy access. Mark each serving bowl with 2 tablespoons of the tare, 1 tablespoon of the pork fat, 1 pinch of the pepper, and 1 pinch of the HonDashi, if using.

4 In a separate large pot affixed with a temperature gauge over medium heat, heat the broth to 190°F (do not boil).

recipe and ingredients continue >

4 pinches HonDashi (optional,
   for a punch of umami)

4 cups tonkotsu broth
   (page 91)

18 ounces fresh ramen
   noodles or 12 ounces dried

5   Slice the ramen eggs in half and set aside.

6   Cook the noodles according to the package
    instructions, minus a few seconds of cooking time,
    as the noodles will continue to cook in the hot broth.

7   When the noodles have about 30 seconds of cooking
    time left, ladle 1½ cups of broth into each bowl. When
    the noodles are done, pull the strainer containing them
    out of the hot water, and using chopsticks, divide the
    noodles as evenly as possible among the serving bowls,
    working as quickly as you can.

8   Once the noodles are in, use chopsticks to lightly stir
    them around, so that broth and fat evenly coat each
    noodle. Then grab as many noodles as possible, pull
    them upward out of the broth, and lay them flat across
    the top, creating a sort of raft on which to lay the
    toppings.

9   To each bowl, add 1 patty of the pork confit,
    1 tablespoon of the scallions, 1 tablespoon of the
    slivered mushrooms, and half an egg. Spoon
    ½ tablespoon of the mayu over the top and
    serve immediately.

Note

This recipe assumes that you have broth, tare, and fats already made. From there, plan to make all the toppings before assembling bowls. (For more on ramen assembly instructions, see page 154.)

EQUIPMENT NEEDED

Full-size baking sheet

Wok or skillet with at least 4-cup capacity

Whisk

Large stockpot with strainer or double boiler with holes

FOR TOPPINGS:

4 slices Soy Pork Belly (page 132)

1 cup fresh or frozen corn kernels

1½ teaspoons canola oil (or other high-heat neutral oil)

4 pats of unsalted butter

2 Ramen Eggs (page 148)

1 cup mung bean sprouts

4 tablespoons thinly sliced scallions (green parts only)

FOR RAMEN:

3 tablespoons pork fat (page 105)

8 tablespoons Miso Tare (page 117; best made at least 1 day in advance)

4 cups tonkotsu broth (page 91)

MISO RAMEN

// MAKES 4 BOWLS

By emulsifying the miso into your broth, you get a silky gravy-like broth that is the richest of all ramen. This is what I crave on really cold days in the dead of winter.

1 Preheat the oven to 375°F.

2 In a sauté pan over medium-high heat, sear the pork belly on both sides to give it some color and set aside.

3 On a baking sheet, toss the corn in the oil and spread it out in an even layer. Roast the corn for 15 minutes or until it reaches your desired level of caramelization.

4 In a wok over high heat, heat 1 tablespoon of the pork fat. Using a whisk, stir the tare into the wok. Watch carefully and work quickly to ensure that it does not burn. Cook until you begin to smell the aroma of miso.

5 Add the broth to the wok, whisking, and bring it to a boil.

ASSEMBLY:

6 Fill your biggest pot three-quarters full with water over high heat to bring the water to a boil, ideally with a strainer (or double boiler with holes) that fits into it. Meanwhile, make sure your serving bowls and all toppings, tare, and fats are laid out for easy access. Mark each serving bowl with ½ tablespoon of the pork fat, 1 pinch of the pepper, and 1 pinch of the HonDashi, if using.

7 Slice the ramen eggs in half and set aside.

8 Cook the noodles according to the package instructions, minus a few seconds of cooking time, as the noodles will continue to cook in the hot broth.

recipe and ingredients continue >

4 pinches ground white
pepper

4 pinches HonDashi (optional,
for a punch of umami)

18 ounces fresh ramen
noodles or 12 ounces dried

9   When the noodles have about 30 seconds of cooking
time left, ladle 1½ cups of broth into each bowl. When
the noodles are done, pull the strainer containing them
out of the hot water, and using chopsticks, divide the
noodles as evenly as possible among the serving bowls,
working as quickly as you can.

10 Once the noodles are in, use chopsticks to lightly stir
them around, so that the broth and fat evenly coat
each noodle. Then grab as many noodles as possible,
pull them upward out of the broth, and lay them flat
across the top, creating a sort of raft on which to lay
the toppings.

11 To each bowl, add 1 slice of the pork belly, half an egg,
¼ cup of the corn, and ¼ cup of the bean sprouts
and one pat of butter. Finish with 1 tablespoon of the
scallions and serve immediately.

TERMINOLOGY FOR RAMEN GAWKERS

There is no one standardized classification system for the thousands of ramen styles
that have been created since the fifties. To help you navigate the crowded field, here
are the definitions of some of the terms you might come across in the nomenclature.
Remember, there are no rules, just guidelines. This list will help you as you "ramen gawk"
online or in ramen shops.

Assari denotes a light-style broth,
like a shio.

Kotteri is a heavier-style ramen, like a
tonkotsu. In many tonkotsu shops, you
can order the bowl "kotteri," which would
mean a more concentrated broth, with
fatback speckles floating in it for added
richness.

Double soup simply means the blending
of two types of soup to make a bowl.
A shio with dashi is a double soup.

Gyokai is used to describe the addition
of a fish or shellfish to the broth for
a deeper, richer, "funkier" flavor
(e.g., gyokai tonkotsu).

Brian MacDuckston (Ramen Adventures)

\\\

Brian is an American who has been living in Japan for over ten years. In that time he has become one of the most well-known English-speaking ramen critics anywhere. Follow him at @ramenadventures for daily bouts of ramen jealousy and inspiration.

\\\

Where was your first official bowl of ramen on record?

My first bowl was at a touristy spot in Ikebukuro, Tokyo, called Mutekiya. Creamy tonkotsu soup that hooked me instantly.

What made you want to start Ramen Adventures?

At the time (late 2008) there was very little in the way of English-language resources for someone who wanted great ramen. Guidebooks focused on convenient chains, and the Japanese media was all in, well, Japanese.

What's your "I can eat it every day" style of ramen?

A lighter shoyu style. After a bowl like that, I don't feel weighed down. Thick ramen induces naps!

What about your "once in a while I have to have it" style of ramen?

Junk-style. It is an uncommon style mostly reserved for Saitama Prefecture. Soupless noodles hit with heavy liquid seasoning, pork back fat, multiple styles of chashu pork, raw garlic, grated cheese, some kind of crunchy chip or cracker, and whatever else the shop master thinks junk means.

What are the first things you look for in a good bowl of ramen?

Nice salty impact with deep flavors, followed by a smooth umami aftertaste.

What do you think the biggest differences are between ramen in the U.S. and ramen in Japan?

The Japanese have umami down to a science. A bowl of ramen has all these different ingredients that give umami: kelp, dried fish, soy sauce, etc. In Japan, the variety of these ingredients is insane. A chef has hundreds of options, while I feel like an American chef only has access to a handful.

What's the most extreme interpretation of ramen that you have eaten? Can it go too far and break too many rules?

There are some pretty horrible bowls in Japan. One guy puts an ice cream cone in it. These are outliers, though, and probably only succeed because the shop has rent control from one hundred years ago and the owner doesn't care about making money. Honestly, I don't know. That said, many good shops will do interesting gentei (limited) bowls that push the boundaries. Gold-dusted uni ramen, anyone?

What's the ramen secret you wish everyone could know?

Eat your ramen quickly and as soon as it is placed in front of you. Hot and fresh is the only way. People, Americans especially, can get angry when you tell them how to eat, but if you let your ramen sit around, it becomes garbage.

Where in the world (outside of Japan) do you see the most exciting ramen being created?

The scene in New York is legit. There is room for many more shops, but people's interest is high, which I like.

NEXT-LEVEL RAMEN RECIPES

11

Training wheels are off now; it's time to experiment. Have you made stock and tare already?

These recipes are some of the best "limited edition" ramen we have at the shop. I have even taken some of these recipes and continued to morph them. I had some Curry Shio Tare left over that I added to a veg broth to make an all-veg ramen.

Again, use these as a starting point and get creative.

Post a picture on Instagram to show me your bowl and tag us at #ramenotakucookbook!

Note

This recipe assumes that you have broth, tare, and fats already made. From there, plan to make all the toppings before assembling bowls. (For more on ramen assembly instructions, see page 154.)

EQUIPMENT NEEDED

Small saucepan

Whisk

Medium sauté pan

Large stockpot with strainer or double boiler with holes

Large pot for broth

FOR RAMEN:

8 tablespoons Shio Tare (page 119; best made at least 1 day in advance)

2 tablespoons Japanese curry powder (like S&B curry powder)

4 tablespoons Sumac Chicken Fat (page 102)

4 cups chintan broth (page 82)

2 cups dashi broth (page 97; must be made 2 days in advance)

18 ounces fresh ramen noodles or 12 ounces dried

FOR TOPPINGS:

5 tablespoons Japanese curry powder (like S&B curry powder)

CURRY SHIO RAMEN

// MAKES 4 BOWLS

I'm obsessed with Japanese curry, which is served like gravy over rice, but when I started thinking about making a curry ramen, I wanted to use curry as a dry spice, rather than a soupy gravy, so it becomes a part of the seasoning. In this recipe, curry spice tare combined with the citrusy sumac chicken fat in the tare and a broth made from a combination of chintan and dashi broths make for a lighter, tangier bowl. I finish the bowl with curry-crusted seared shrimp and shredded cabbage. It's become one of my all-time favorite ramen.

1 Make the curry tare: In a small saucepan over very low heat, combine the shio tare and curry powder and simmer for 15 to 20 minutes, whisking and tasting often, until the flavors have come together. Remove the pot from the heat and set aside.

2 Make the shrimp topping: In a small bowl, mix together the curry powder, salt, shichimi togarashi, garlic powder, and onion powder. Add the shrimp and toss evenly to coat.

3 In a medium sauté pan over medium-high heat, heat the oil. Sear the shrimp for 2 minutes per side, or until pink, then set aside.

ASSEMBLY:

4 Fill your biggest pot three-quarters full with water over high heat to bring the water to a boil, ideally with a strainer (or double boiler with holes) that fits into it. Meanwhile, make sure your serving bowls and all toppings, tare, and fats are laid out for easy access. Mark each serving bowl with 2 tablespoons of the curry tare and 1 tablespoon of sumac chicken fat.

recipe and ingredients continue >

5 tablespoons kosher salt

2 tablespoons shichimi togarashi (red chili spice blend)

1 tablespoon garlic powder

1 tablespoon onion powder

12 medium shrimp, peeled and deveined

1 tablespoon canola oil (or other high-heat neutral oil)

2 Ramen Eggs (page 148)

4 tablespoons thinly sliced scallions (green parts only)

2 cups shredded white or green cabbage

5 In a separate large pot affixed with a temperature gauge over medium heat, combine the chintan and the dashi and heat the broth to 190°F (do not boil).

6 Slice the ramen eggs in half and set aside.

7 Cook the noodles according to the package instructions, minus a few seconds of cooking time, as the noodles will continue to cook in the hot broth.

8 When the noodles have about 30 seconds of cooking time left, ladle 1½ cups of broth into each bowl. When the noodles are done, pull the strainer containing them out of the hot water, and using chopsticks, divide the noodles as evenly as possible among the serving bowls, working as quickly as you can.

9 Once the noodles are in, use chopsticks to lightly stir them around, so that broth and fat evenly coat each noodle. Then grab as many noodles as possible, pull them upward out of the broth, and lay them flat across the top, creating a sort of raft on which to lay the toppings.

10 To each bowl, add 3 seared shrimp, half an egg, 1 tablespoon of the scallions, and ½ cup of the cabbage. Serve immediately.

Note

This recipe assumes that you have broth, tare, and fats already made. From there, plan to make all the toppings before assembling bowls. (For more on ramen assembly instructions, see page 154.)

EQUIPMENT NEEDED

Large stockpot with strainer or double boiler with holes

Large pot for broth

8 tablespoons Shio Tare (page 119)

4 tablespoons chicken fat (page 102)

6 cups paitan broth (page 88)

2 tablespoons unsalted butter (optional)

18 ounces fresh ramen noodles or 12 ounces dried

4 cups Meatball Mix, balled or ground (page 128)

2 Ramen Eggs (page 148)

4 tablespoons thinly sliced scallions (green parts only)

BUTTERED TORI PAITAN RAMEN

// MAKES 4 BOWLS

This is a traditional chicken paitan (cloudy white bone broth) ramen, seasoned with a shio (salt)-based tare plus butter emulsified into the broth and topped with a classic combination of ramen eggs and our ground chicken mix. While porky tonkotsu ramen is becoming increasingly popular in America, tori paitan delivers the same rich, creamy mouthfeel with a cleaner chicken flavor. I personally hope to see it catch on here soon. This paitan is silky and rich, and once you have had a great paitan, you will be fully converted. The butter adds to the silkiness for me, but it is optional here.

ASSEMBLY:

1 Fill your biggest pot three-quarters full with water over high heat to bring the water to a boil, ideally with a strainer (or double boiler with holes) that fits into it.

2 Meanwhile, make sure your serving bowls and all toppings, tare, and fats are laid out for easy access. Mark each serving bowl with 2 tablespoons of the tare and 1 tablespoon of the chicken fat.

3 In a separate large pot affixed with a temperature gauge over medium heat, heat the broth to 190°F (do not boil). Using a hand blender, emulsify the butter into the broth.

4 Slice the ramen eggs in half and set aside.

recipe continues >

5 Cook the noodles according to the package instructions, minus a few seconds of cooking time, as the noodles will continue to cook in the hot broth.

6 When the noodles have about 30 seconds of cooking time left, ladle 1½ cups of broth into each bowl. When the noodles are done, pull the strainer containing them out of the hot water, and using chopsticks, divide the noodles as evenly as possible among the serving bowls, working as quickly as you can.

7 Once the noodles are in, use chopsticks to lightly stir them around, so that broth and fat evenly coat each noodle. Then grab as many noodles as possible, pull them upward out of the broth, and lay them flat across the top, creating a sort of raft on which to lay the toppings.

8 To each bowl, add half an egg, 1 cup of the meatball mix, and 1 tablespoon of the scallions. Serve immediately.

This recipe assumes that you have broth, tare, and fats already made. From there, plan to make all the toppings before assembling bowls. (For more on ramen assembly instructions, see page 154.)

EQUIPMENT NEEDED

Baking dish large enough to fit two full-size chicken breasts

Small cast-iron or heavy skillet

Large stockpot with strainer or double boiler with holes

Large pot for broth

FOR RAMEN:

1 lemon

8 tablespoons Shio Tare (page 119; best made at least 1 day in advance)

4 tablespoons chicken fat (page 102)

6 cups paitan broth (page 88)

18 ounces fresh ramen noodles or 12 ounces dried

FOR TOPPINGS:

2 chicken breasts (or 2 leftover cooked breasts)

2 teaspoons salt

½ cup paitan broth

2 cups thinly sliced hearty green such as mustard greens or collards

4 tablespoons thinly sliced scallions (green parts only)

2 Ramen Eggs (page 148)

LEMON CHICKEN PAITAN

// MAKES 4 BOWLS

Roasted lemony chicken, aka "Lemon Up the Butt Chicken" was one of the first recipes I mastered when I was learning to cook, and to this day it's one of my death-row meals. So when I began my journey as ramen otaku, it only made sense for me to translate my love for lemon chicken into a ramen, and thus, the Lemon Chicken Paitan was born. The charred lemon helps balance the rich paitan chicken broth, and the shredded chicken on top makes great use of any leftover meat you may have.

1   Preheat the oven to 375°F.

2   Make the shredded chicken: If you have leftover cooked breasts from making the broth, simply shred those and move on. If you do not, season the breasts on both sides with the salt. In a baking dish, place the ½ cup paitan and the seasoned chicken, cover with foil, and bake for 30 minutes, or until the juices in the thickest part of the chicken run clear when a knife is inserted. Allow the chicken to rest until it is cool enough to handle, then shred by hand and set aside.

3   Make the charred lemon juice: Cut the lemon in half. Heat a cast-iron skillet over high heat until it reaches its smoke point. Add the lemons, cut side down, and cook until they sizzle and begin to char, about 8 minutes.

4   Let cool, then juice the lemons, straining any seeds or solids. Discard the spent halves and set the juice aside.

5   Blanch the greens: In a large pot over high heat, bring 4 quarts of water to a boil. Prepare an ice bath in a large bowl.

recipe continues >

6 When water is boiling, add the broccolini and cook for about 30 seconds. Immediately plunge the broccolini in the ice water, pat dry, and set aside.

ASSEMBLY:

7 Fill your biggest pot three-quarters full with water over high heat to bring the water to a boil, ideally with a strainer (or double boiler with holes) that fits into it.

8 Meanwhile, make sure your serving bowls and all toppings, tare, and fats are laid out for easy access. Mark each serving bowl with 2 tablespoons of the tare, 1 tablespoon of the chicken fat, and ¼ teaspoon of the charred lemon juice.

9 In a separate large pot affixed with a temperature gauge over medium heat, heat the broth to 190°F (do not boil).

10 Slice the ramen eggs in half and set aside.

11 Cook the noodles according to the package instructions, minus a few seconds of cooking time, as the noodles will continue to cook in the hot broth.

12 When the noodles have about 30 seconds of cooking time left, ladle 1½ cups of broth into each bowl. When the noodles are done, pull the strainer containing them out of the hot water, and using chopsticks, divide the noodles as evenly as possible among the serving bowls, working as quickly as you can.

13 Once the noodles are in, use chopsticks to lightly stir them around, so that broth and fat evenly coat each noodle. Then grab as many noodles as possible, pull them upward out of the broth, and lay them flat across the top, creating a sort of raft on which to lay the toppings.

14 To each bowl, add 1 cup of the shredded chicken, ½ cup of the broccolini, 1 tablespoon of the scallions, and half an egg. Serve immediately.

This recipe assumes that you have broth, tare, and fats already made. From there, plan to make all the toppings before assembling bowls. (For more on ramen assembly instructions, see page 154.)

EQUIPMENT NEEDED

Wok or skillet with at least 4-cup capacity

Strainer

Full-size baking sheet

Whisk

Large stockpot with strainer or double boiler with holes

FOR TOPPINGS:

2 cups ground pork

2 tablespoons canola oil (or other high-heat neutral oil)

2 teaspoons salt

2 cups fresh or frozen corn kernels

2 cups chopped kimchi

4 tablespoons thinly sliced scallions (green parts only)

2 Ramen Eggs (page 148)

FOR RAMEN:

8 tablespoons Spicy Miso Tare (page 118; best made at least 1 day in advance)

4 tablespoons Garlic Chicken Fat (page 102)

4 pinches of ground white pepper

SPICY MISO RAMEN

// MAKES 4 BOWLS

Every shop that makes tonkotsu has a spicy version. I doubled down and made my spicy tonkotsu a miso soup as well. I will never take this ramen off the menu at Otaku; it's a fan favorite for sure. The tare is medium on the spice, but you can bump that up with extra sambal to give it an extra punch. Like the standard miso, the key to really making this ramen sing is cooking the miso and emulsifying it with the fat and then the stock. I call for chicken fat in this version, but you can really use any kind of animal fat. As a matter of fact, bacon grease is fantastic here. Just adds another level of flavor.

1   Preheat the oven to 375°F.

2   Make the ground pork: Heat your wok over medium heat, add 1 tablespoon canola oil, and heat until the oil reaches its smoke point. Stir in the pork until cooked through and season with the salt. Strain the pork, reserving the pork fat in the wok.

3   On a baking sheet, toss the corn in 1 tablespoon canola oil the and spread it out in an even layer. Roast the corn for 15 minutes, or until it reaches your desired level of caramelization. Set aside.

4   Heat the reserved pork fat in the wok over high heat. Add the tare to the wok and use a whisk to mix. Watch carefully and work quickly to ensure that it does not burn. Cook until you begin to smell the miso.

5   Add the broth, whisking well, and bring the mixture to a boil.

recipe and ingredients continue >

18 ounces fresh ramen
noodles or 12 ounces dried

6 cups tonkotsu broth
(page 91)

ASSEMBLY:

6 Fill your biggest pot three-quarters full with water over high heat to bring the water to a boil, ideally with a strainer (or double boiler with holes) that fits into it.

7 Meanwhile, make sure your serving bowls and all toppings, tare, and fats are laid out for easy access. Mark each serving bowl with 1 tablespoon of the chicken fat and 1 pinch of the pepper.

8 Slice the ramen eggs in half and set aside.

9 Cook the noodles according to the package instructions, minus a few seconds of cooking time, as the noodles will continue to cook in the hot broth.

10 When the noodles have about 30 seconds of cooking time left, ladle 1½ cups of broth into each bowl. When the noodles are done, pull the strainer containing them out of the hot water, and using chopsticks, divide the noodles as evenly as possible among the serving bowls, working as quickly as you can.

11 Once the noodles are in, use chopsticks to lightly stir them around, so that broth and fat evenly coat each noodle. Then grab as many noodles as possible, pull them upward out of the broth, and lay them flat across the top, creating a sort of raft on which to lay the toppings.

12 To each bowl, add 1 cup of the ground pork, ½ cup of the chopped kimchi, ½ cup of the roasted corn, and half an egg. Finish with 1 tablespoon of the scallions and serve immediately.

Note

This recipe assumes that you have broth, tare, and fats already made. From there, plan to make all the toppings before assembling bowls. (For more on ramen assembly instructions, see page 154.)

EQUIPMENT NEEDED

Large pot for blanching greens

Large bowl for ice bath

Large stockpot with strainer or double boiler with holes

Large pot for broth

Whisk

FOR TOPPINGS:

4 cups shredded Chicken Confit (page 127)

1 cup thinly sliced leafy greens, such as collard or mustard greens

1 cup diced carrots (½-inch dice)

4 tablespoons thinly sliced scallions (green parts only)

2 Ramen Eggs (page 148)

FOR RAMEN:

8 tablespoons Shio Tare (page 119; best made at least 1 day in advance)

4 tablespoons Ginger Scallion Oil (page 106)

2 teaspoons toasted sesame oil

EGG DROP SHIO RAMEN

// MAKES 4 BOWLS

I have such fond memories of egg drop soup at my favorite Chinese restaurants. It always burns my mouth, too. The first time I had a really great shio ramen it made me think of the viscosity of an egg drop soup. And knowing now what we do about the impact of Chinese cooking methods on ramen, this idea seemed like it made sense. This ramen is egg drop soup with ramen noodles in it and a balance of great umami. You are welcome.

1 Bring the shredded chicken to room temperature.

2 Blanch the greens and carrots: In a large pot, bring 4 quarts of water to a boil. Prepare an ice bath in a large bowl. When the water is boiling, add the greens and carrots and cook for about 30 seconds. Immediately plunge the greens and carrots in the ice water, pat dry, and set aside.

ASSEMBLY:

3 Fill your biggest pot three-quarters full with water over high heat to bring the water to a boil, ideally with a strainer (or double boiler with holes) that fits into it.

4 Meanwhile, make sure your serving bowls and all toppings, tare, and fats are laid out for easy access. Mark each serving bowl with 2 tablespoons of the tare, 1 tablespoon of the Ginger Scallion Oil, ½ teaspoon of the sesame oil, and 1 pinch of the pepper.

5 In a separate large pot affixed with a temperature gauge over medium heat, heat the broth to 190°F (do not boil). Add ¼ cup hot broth to the 1 tablespoon

recipe and ingredients continue >

1 teaspoon ground black
   pepper

4 cups chintan broth
   (page 82)

2 cups dashi broth (page 97)

2 large raw eggs beaten
   together

1 tablespoon cornstarch

18 ounces fresh or 12 ounces
   dried ramen noodles

of cornstarch to create a slurry and add mix into the broth. Mix the remaining 1 tablespoon cornstarch with the beaten egg and pour into hot soup through the tynes of a fork, stirring with a whisk in a clockwise motion to create the egg shards in the soup.

6 Slice the ramen eggs in half and set aside.

7 Cook the noodles according to the package instructions, minus a few seconds of cooking time, as the noodles will continue to cook in the hot broth.

8 When the noodles have about 30 seconds of cooking time left, ladle 1½ cups of broth into each bowl. When the noodles are done, pull the strainer containing them out of the hot water, and using chopsticks, divide the noodles as evenly as possible among the serving bowls, working as quickly as you can.

9 Once the noodles are in, use chopsticks to lightly stir them around, so that broth and fat evenly coat each noodle. Then grab as many noodles as possible, pull them upward out of the broth, and lay them flat across the top, creating a sort of raft on which to lay the toppings.

10 To each bowl, add 1 cup of the shredded chicken, ½ cup of the mixed greens and carrots, 1 tablespoon of the scallions, and half an egg. Serve immediately.

Note

This recipe assumes that you have broth, tare, and fats already made. From there, plan to make all the toppings before assembling bowls. (For more on ramen assembly instructions, see page 154.)

EQUIPMENT NEEDED

Small cast-iron or heavy skillet

Large stockpot with strainer or double boiler with holes

Large pot for broth

FOR TOPPINGS

2 tablespoons canola oil (or other high-heat neutral oil)

4 cups riced cauliflower

2 tablespoons Spicy Miso Tare (page 118)

2 Ramen Eggs (page 148)

4 tablespoons thinly sliced scallions (green parts only)

2 tablespoons Rayu (page 109)

FOR RAMEN

8 tablespoons Miso Tare (page 117)

6 cups Vegetable Stock (page 98)

18 ounces fresh ramen noodles or 12 ounces dried

CAULIFLOWER TANTANMEN

// MAKES 4 BOWLS

The combination of sesame and chili oil defines a "tantanmen," which is a derivation of the Chinese Dandan noodle dish. I love this ramen for the flavors and the heartiness, which is hard to do without animal fat. A traditional tantanmen uses ground pork as the topping, but here we use riced cauliflower, which really works great as a topping.

1 Heat a medium cast-iron skillet over medium-high heat with canola oil, add the riced cauliflower, and saute until cooked through, for 5 to 8 minutes. Add the spicy miso tare and mix until well blended. Set aside.

2 Fill your biggest pot ¾ with water over high heat to bring water to a boil, ideally with a strainer (or double boiler with holes) that fits into it.

3 Meanwhile, make sure your serving bowls and all toppings, tare, and fats are laid out for easy access. Mark each serving bowl with 2 tablespoons of the tare.

4 In a separate large pot affixed with a temperature gauge over medium heat, heat the broth to a boil.

5 Slice the ramen eggs in half and set aside.

6 Cook the noodles according to the package instructions, minus a few seconds of cooking time, as the noodles will continue to cook in the hot broth.

7 When the noodles have about 30 seconds of cooking time left, ladle 1½ cups of broth into each bowl and whisk tare in until totally emulsified. When the noodles

recipe continues >

are done, pull the strainer containing them out of the hot water, and using chopsticks, divide the noodles as evenly as possible among the serving bowls, working as quickly as you can.

8   Once the noodles are in, use chopsticks to lightly stir them around, so that broth and fat evenly coat each noodle. Then grab as many noodles as possible, pull them upward out of the broth, and lay them flat across the top, creating a sort of raft on which to lay the toppings.

9   To each bowl, add 1 cup of the cauliflower mixture, 1 tablespoon of the scallions, and half an egg. Add ½ tablespoon of rayu to each bowl with a spoon. Serve immediately.

Large bowl for sauce

Large stockpot with strainer or double boiler with holes

Large bowl for ice bath

Large skillet for cooking pork

TANTAN SAUCE:

1 cup white miso

½ cup gochujang (Korean chili paste)

1 cup dashi broth

¼ cup tahini

¼ cup Rayu (page 109)

¼ cup sambal

GROUND PORK:

1 tablespoon canola oil

¼ cup diced shallot

¼ cup peeled and diced ginger

2 cups ground pork

FOR RAMEN:

18 ounces fresh ramen noodles or 12 ounces dried (thicker is better for this dish)

4 teaspoons toasted sesame seeds

4 tablespoons thinly sliced scallions (green parts only)

TANTAN MAZEMEN

// SERVES 4

This is our most requested mazemen on the menu at the shop. I serve it cold on the summer menu, but it can be served warm as well. The tantan flavor profile of chili and sesame came from China and is mostly seen in ramen as a tantanmen and served as a brothed hot ramen. I took that concept and made it into a cold sauce.

I have always loved the deep dank flavors of the Chinese exports that line the shelves at the Asian market. To me, that musty aroma of dried and fermented chiles in a dish is strangely satisfying. This sauce was the simplest version of that notion. You can serve it cold (as outlined in this recipe) or warm, and it will become a staple in your fridge. We have been known to serve it with roast chicken at my house—it works on anything.

1 Prepare the sauce: In a large bowl, mix together all the ingredients. Set aside.

2 Fill your biggest pot three-quarters full with water over high heat to bring the water to a boil, ideally with a strainer (or double boiler with holes) that fits into it.

3 Prepare an ice bath in a large bowl.

4 Cook the noodles according to the package instructions, then quickly plunge them into the ice bath to stop them from cooking further.

5 In a large skillet over medium-high heat, heat the oil. Sauté the ginger and shallot for 3 to 5 minutes, until soft. Add the pork and sauté until cooked through, about 10 minutes

6 Add the noodles to the bowl with the tantan sauce and mix. Portion the noodles evenly among 4 bowls, and top each bowl with ¾ cup of the ground pork mixture, 1 teaspoon of the sesame seeds, and 1 tablespoon of the scallions. Serve immediately.

Large bowl for dressing

Large stockpot with strainer
 or double boiler with holes

Large bowl for ice bath

FOR DRESSING

1 cup ponzu

4 tablespoons sesame oil

1 teaspoon peeled and freshly
 grated ginger

Juice of 1 lemon

1 teaspoon toasted sesame
 seeds

FOR RAMEN:

18 ounces fresh ramen
 noodles or 12 ounces dried
 (thicker is better for this
 dish)

FOR TOPPINGS:

½ cup hijiki seaweed,
 rehydrated in 2 cups of
 hot water for 15 minutes
 and drained

½ cup sugar snap peas, cut on
 the bias

3 eggs, mixed and cooked into
 a thin omelet, rolled, and
 cut into threads

1 cup sliced Pickled Shiitakes
 (page 142)

1 cup julienned cucumber

1 tablespoon thinly sliced
 scallions (green parts only)

1 teaspoon black sesame seeds

HIYASHI CHUKA (VEGETABLE MAZEMEN)

// SERVES 4

This dish is traditional and yet its creation stems from my obsession with chopped salad. Stay with me . . . The most popular cold noodle ramen dish in the summer in Japan is hiyashi chuka, which resembles a Cobb salad: noodles tossed in ponzu and topped with chopped veggies, cooked egg, and sometimes even ham. I always loved the idea of the dish, but it simply never delivered. I also have a major issue with being given a salad I have to mix up myself, which means you never really get one perfectly seasoned bite. So here you go: a chopped-salad version of a hiyashi chuka.

1 Make the dressing: Whisk together all the dressing ingredients. Set aside.

2 Fill your biggest pot three-quarters full with water over high heat to bring the water to a boil, ideally with a strainer (or double boiler with holes) that fits into it.

3 Prepare an ice bath in a large bowl.

4 Cook the noodles according to the package instructions, then quickly plunge them into the ice bath to stop them from cooking further. Drain.

5 In a small bowl, toss together the hijiki and snap peas. Portion the noodles, toppings, and dressing evenly among 4 bowls. Serve immediately.

EQUIPMENT NEEDED

Large sauté pan

Sheet pan

Large saucepan

Whisk

Large stockpot with strainer or double boiler with holes

FOR THE RAMEN:

2 cups Soy-Braised Mushrooms (page 198)

1 cup Maz Sauce (recipe follows)

½ cup julienned pickled mustard greens

20 ounces thicker ramen noodles, cooked

½ cup grated Parmesan cheese

¼ cup toasted white sesame seeds, for garnish

4 teaspoons shichimi togarashi, for garnish

4 slow-cooked (see Note) or poached eggs

¼ cup scallion threads (green part only), for garnish

SOY-BRAISED SHIITAKE MAZ AND CHEESE

// SERVES 4

You will never crave store-bought mac and cheese again after making this. The combo of shiitake, shoyu, and parm is umami central. This was the first ramen one of our chefs at the shop ever created and it just stuck. I've never met anyone who doesn't like this combination of flavors.

1 In a large sauté pan over high heat, combine the mushrooms, sauce, and mustard greens and bring to a boil.

2 Add the noodles and toss until coated and the sauce begins to bubble. There should be very little to no excess sauce left in the pan, as it should all be coating the noodles.

3 Remove the pan from the heat and add the cheese. Stir until the cheese is evenly distributed.

4 Divide the noodles among 4 bowls for serving. To each bowl, add 1 pinch of the sesame seeds, 1 teaspoon of the togarashi, 1 of the eggs, and a pinch of the scallions.

recipe and ingredients continue >

2 tablespoons vegetable oil

10 cups shiitake mushrooms, roughly chopped

1 cup Vegetable Stock (page 98)

½ cup soy sauce

1 tablespoon sesame oil

2 tablespoons sake

1 tablespoon plus 1½ teaspoons dark brown sugar

1 teaspoon ground white pepper

SOY-BRAISED MUSHROOMS

// MAKES 4 CUPS

1 In a large saucepan over high heat, heat the oil. When the oil begins to smoke, add the mushrooms and sauté until they're caramelized, about 10 minutes. And don't forget, as Julia Child says, "don't crowd the mushrooms." Work in batches to ensure you can caramelize and do not sweat the mushrooms.

2 Stir in the stock, soy sauce, sesame oil, sake, sugar, and pepper and reduce the heat to medium. Cook until most of the liquid has reduced. Remove the pan from the heat and transfer the mixture to a sheet pan to allow the mushrooms to cool.

3 Transfer the mushrooms to an airtight container and store it in the refrigerator.

3 cups Vegetable Stock
(page 98)

1½ cups soy sauce

6 tablespoons sake

¼ cup dark brown sugar

1 tablespoon ground white
pepper

1 tablespoon cornstarch

1 tablespoon water

MAZ SAUCE

// MAKES 4 CUPS

1 In a large saucepan over high heat, combine the stock, soy sauce, sake, sugar, and pepper and bring the mixture to a boil.

2 In a small bowl, mix together the cornstarch and water to form a slurry.

3 Add the cornstarch slurry in a slow stream to the boiling liquid, whisking constantly and vigorously until the liquid begins to thicken. Remove the pan from the heat, transfer the sauce to an airtight container, and store it in the refrigerator.

Note

To make slow-cooked eggs: Set up a sous vide bath at 149°F and slow-cook your eggs in the shell for 45 minutes. Keep them in their shells until you're ready to serve—or cook poached eggs.

ACKNOWLEDGMENTS

This journey has become a part of me, of who I am from the inside out, and because of it, I live an incredible life. Without the support of the people below this project would never have seen the light of day.

To the people and city of Nashville, thank you from the bottom of my heart for supporting this little noodle dream. You are hungrier than I thought, and it is an honor to feed you all.

Matt, this book literally would not exist today unless you had called me and pushed me to push myself. Your friendship and guidance has been incredible. I will follow you anywhere.

Angela, Jamie, and Anne, you pushed and wrote and analyzed with me to get here and I am so proud of what we have created.

Miranda, you threw out the challenge, I took it.

Erik, you pushed me out of my comfort zone and gave me permission to just do it. Thank you.

Charlie, Daniel, Scott, Tony, Bridgette, and William, many of these recipes were created with you, and I simply would not have had this opportunity without your hard work, love of ramen, and support.

To the "Pink Lemonadies" Michelle and Emily, it has been such a joy to make this book with you. Your vision, support, and hard work are the meat and bones of this project.

A very special thank-you to Kenshiro Uki, Sun Noodle, Shigetoshi Nakamura, and Yuji Haraguchi for accepting me with open arms into the ramen community and sharing your knowledge with me.

Mom and Dad, who are always there for me without question or judgment. I love you both so much and know that you are the greatest gift life has bestowed on me. Thank you for everything you have done to make my life glorious.

Augusta, without your love of ramen, your gift of words and humor, and your love for me we would never have taken this crazy ride. Thanks for being my slurping sidekick.

Brad, you are my partner in every way, and I cannot imagine life without your unending support and love. To many more projects and a lot more travel, laughter, food, and fun. Thank you for everything you do to support me.

INDEX